WHEN GOD CALLS, HOW DO YOU ANSWER?

Becoming a Spiritual Entrepreneur

ROBERT WESTHEIMER

 radiant star books

radiant star books
AN IMPRINT OF **bright sky press**

2365 Rice Blvd., Suite 202
Houston, Texas 77005

10   9   8   7   6   5   4   3   2   1

Library of Congress Cataloging-in-Publication Data

Westheimer, Robert.
When God calls, how do you answer? : becoming a spiritual entrepreneur /
Robert Westheimer. -- 1 [edition].
       pages cm
ISBN 978-1-942945-12-3 (alk. paper)
1. Christian life. 2. Risk taking (Psychology)--Religious aspects--Christianity.
3. Adventure and adventurers--Miscellanea. I. Title.

BV4509.5.W434 2015
248.4--dc23   2015032301

Editorial Direction: Lucy Herring Chambers
Managing Editor: Lauren Adams
Designer: Marla Y. Garcia

Printed in Canada through Friesens

"I am looking for someone to share in an adventure that I am arranging, and it's very difficult to find anyone."
"I should think so—in these parts! We are plain quiet folk and have no use for adventures. Nasty disturbing uncomfortable things! Make you late for dinner!"

THE HOBBIT

HAVE YOU BEEN CALLED?

Have you been called to a spiritual experience that you can't quite explain? Are you feeling drawn toward something new and strange, something totally off your radar?

If so, you might just be a *spiritual entrepreneur* being called to a *spiritual adventure.* Can the words "spiritual" and "entrepreneur" even be used in the same sentence? Yes, they can. And those words just might apply to *you* as God calls you to join Him in an adventure of His making.

But what is a spiritual adventure? It's a journey, a plunge into something with unknown factors, something new, something different, and something beyond your comfort zone. It is an undertaking that is admittedly not without a degree of risk. While a spiritual adventure can make you uncomfortable and test your faith, it can also be profoundly enriching and fun.

Spiritual adventures come in all shapes and sizes. But each one begins the same: with a calling from God. We might think that God calls only pastors and "giants" of the faith and not ordinary people like you and me. But scripture and the history of the church teach otherwise. At one time or another, His call comes to each one of us. And over the centuries of our faith, some of the most ordinary among us have heard the greatest calls.

But what exactly is a calling from God? And to what are we called? Actually, we can be called to almost anything. Perhaps you've been called to an idea for a new faith-based business, grounded in Christian values. Or perhaps your call is to start or join an organization or ministry whose mission is to serve others in the name of Christ. Your calling could even be to engage in a relationship that has a deeply spiritual dimension, or to take part in a mission trip to a place you might otherwise never choose to visit.

Whatever it is, if you are a Christian, you either have been or will be called. Yes, you. Not just a few leaders or giants of the faith. Each of us is called. So whatever your calling is, at its core, it is a call to follow Christ.

Whoever serves me must follow me, and where I am, there will my servant be also.

JOHN 12:26

Over and over in scripture, Jesus calls His disciples to "come and see" and to follow Him. In the same way, He calls to us today. But to where? To what kind of service? Will there be risk? Suffering? Uncertainty?

When we first hear this call, we want answers, but He offers us few— if any. Even if we try to hide from His calling, God continues to nudge us, to draw us, and persistently whisper to us.

If you are hearing that persistent whisper, and if you cannot rid yourself of the sense of being called, this book is for you. Will it help?

It will if you already feel engaged in a spiritual adventure but are frustrated by your inability to express it to anyone. It will if you have no idea why you are embarking on that adventure and feel totally unprepared and alone. It will if an unspoken voice is pulling you, or if you just woke up in the middle of something and aren't sure how you landed there.

If you are no longer willing to hide from that persistent whisper and you feel a strange sense of belonging to something that you never dreamed of, this book is for you.

This book is not a "how to" book. It is a "with you" book. It is meant to give you a window into the claim our Lord has placed on you. Whether you acknowledge it or not, a claim *has* been placed on your life. His claim on your life may be short-lived or it may last forever. Whichever it is, it cannot be denied and you know it. In a way, you have been captured.

My hope is that this book will give you a healthy dose of encouragement. Read it a bit at a time and see if you feel a little less alone, a little more encouraged, a little less afraid.

So who am I? I am one who has heard the call, more like a whisper than a trumpet call. Our Lord has engaged me in something not of my own making, a call "through a glass darkly" to witness to Him by serving the poor. Like you, I am one called to something I am not sure of, a journey without a clear destination, a path with no road signs.

Perhaps we are like the pilgrims walking to Emmaus on Easter afternoon. Did they know why they were going to Emmaus? Was their trip an attempt to escape the horror of Good Friday? To get out of town to try to sort out what happened? Luke doesn't tell us. My belief is that, like you and me, they were walking with absolutely no goal in mind, only to discover that their goal wasn't a destination at all. But, instead, it was an encounter with the risen Christ.

A NOTE ON TERMINOLOGY

God is not limited by the English language, or by any human language for that matter. I use the terms "adventure," "ministry," "experience," "calling," and a few others interchangeably. And you may likewise struggle to give a label or name to your calling from God. That's okay. God's callings do not fit neatly into human categories, nor are they easily described in human terms. Perhaps that's why Jesus chose to speak in parables and metaphors.

So as you read, feel free to substitute whatever term best fits your particular calling. You might even try, if you can, to suspend your very human propensity to label, categorize, and classify, and let God speak to your heart in *His* language, the language of love.

Many people mistake our work for our vocation.
Our vocation is the love of Jesus.
MOTHER TERESA

TABLE OF CONTENTS

MY STORY

When you hear the term *entrepreneur,* what comes to mind? For many, it suggests images of someone tinkering in a garage and coming up with a dazzling idea that earns millions overnight. Or someone whose new product wows a "shark tank" of successful business people, then sweeps the market before the corporate giants can react.

An entrepreneur is someone with unshakeable self-confidence who is willing to take big risks. The rest of us might stretch ourselves to tiptoe outside our comfort zones, but entrepreneurs don't even appear to have comfort zones.

The term "entrepreneur" never applied to me. It didn't even come close. Yet, now I consider myself a "spiritual entrepreneur," though you'd never know it from my résumé. My résumé shows someone who was a CPA/business consultant for twenty-eight years, someone who never took even one new product to market, and who wasn't paid to act boldly. I was someone who was rewarded for managing—not taking—risks. Ultimately, you'd find someone who was quite adept at staying safely inside his comfort zone. My self-confidence never approached "unshakeable."

For over forty years my spiritual life followed an equally safe path: belonging to a nice, suburban, white collar, Presbyterian church, serving on all the right committees and teaching second grade Sunday School. My spiritual ticket was punched in all the right places, and it showed no traces of boldness, risk-taking, or new ideas. Changing pews at Sunday worship seemed risky enough to me.

But all along, there had been a whisper, one that intensified as the years passed. The whisper wasn't audible. It was more of a feeling, a nudge to something more, something new, something that went beyond. And what's more, it came from inside. Inside? Is that possible?

I didn't try to tune it out. It was such a pleasant whisper—not threatening in any way, though very persistent. In the back of my mind I knew that, someday, I was destined to act on it. Someday, I would live out its message. Someday. But not now.

Someday finally came, though not in a manner I could ever have expected. It began with my prayer life and my Bible study. To say that they were flat and lifeless would be charitable. In fact, they were so moribund that I actually began to pray that these spiritual disciplines might come to life.

And guess what? They didn't.

I prayed those prayers for over ten years. And then, as if scales had fallen off my eyes, things changed. My prayer time came alive and I began to experiment with silent prayer, prayer on my knees, and contemplative prayer. And at the same time, I began a *lectio divina* style of reading the Bible. Covering just a few verses a day, and journaling what they spoke to me connected me to scripture in a way that I had never before thought possible.

Next, as these changes complemented what appeared as disasters elsewhere, I experienced a sort of convergence. My position as a partner with the accounting firm Arthur Andersen & Co. suddenly ended when the firm was brought down over the Enron scandal. Two weeks later, I was diagnosed with cancer and quickly had surgery to remove a tumor. It seemed that fate was playing out its hand just as I was coming alive spiritually.

I somehow knew that the time had come to bring that inaudible whisper to life. And, almost as if on cue, opportunities began to present themselves. Someday had arrived!

Individuals appeared in my life, presenting new possibilities for ministry. I leapt at the opportunity to help plant new churches, with no conception of the difficulty. Encouragement flowed from all sides and relationships unlike any I'd ever known were being built. These were deep, spirit-filled relationships, so different from the superficial acquaintances of my business life.

Alas, the church planting effort did not turn out well. Clearly, I had much to learn, mostly about how important it is to suspend our worldly definitions of success and failure. Our Lord's Kingdom recognizes no such definitions. I learned that what looked to me like institutional failure was actually saturated with individual stories of grace and faith that might otherwise have gone unnoticed.

Even in my self-assessed failure, the persistent whisper never left; so despite my self-condemnation, I decided that if He still believed in me, then perhaps I should believe in myself. Something more lay ahead. But what?

It's human nature to look as far as we can see down the road into the future, hoping to get a glimpse of what our Lord has in store for us. We strain for a vision of what is to come. What I had to learn (again and again) is that our Lord doesn't come to us down the straight line of a highway to the future; instead He comes from our blind spot, not from the frontal view of our vision, but from around the next corner. He surprises us in the immediacy of the present, just as the bridegroom appeared unexpectedly at midnight in Matthew 25:6. Hard as we may try, we just cannot anticipate Him.

What I didn't understand at the time was that the second (and final) church plant was to give birth to a new 501(c)(3) organization. All of the work, all of the prayer, all of the relationship-building around church-planting was preparing me to start the Christ-centered ministry known today as Newspring. I found myself committed to it before any thoughts of caution could form. By that point, my comfort zone had evaporated.

And He didn't stop there. No, He continued to bring opportunities and more importantly, to bring people around this new enterprise, and around me personally. His faithfulness is without peer.

The experience of starting Newspring is the basis for what I share here. People frequently ask me how this organization came about. They expect my story to be quite linear, starting with a dream or vision that led to a well thought-out plan, and, finally, to fruition as a successful ministry. However, in our Lord's spiritual realm, it doesn't actually work that way. I have worried that my story disappoints listeners when I say that I never had a vision for this ministry, and that I stepped into it without knowing exactly what it was all about. But God knew, and as it turns out, that's good enough for me. He has finally (mostly) broken my need to know and control everything.

I always envied people who had riveting stories of God rescuing them from addictions, saving them from financial disasters, or redeeming them from all sorts of terrible sins. My life was so bland, so unremarkable, dry as toast. I had no such story.

But no longer. That's what I am most grateful for: our Lord has taken me through good times and trying times, He has shown me amazing things, and He has used me in ways that I might not have understood or appreciated at first. In short, He has given me my story—His story, actually, with me playing my part.

That is what these pages are all about: how God can give each of us our own unique, personal story, encompassing highs and lows, successes and failures, but always revealing His remarkable love and faithfulness. All we have to do is to listen for His whisper.

And say yes.

I.
WHO ARE
YOU (REALLY)?

J ust like you, I have taken psychological profiles and ap-
titude tests for career potential. I am sure that we can
learn from them. But just the same, they tend to give us
a dualistic view of ourselves. Some attributes are stronger while others
are weaker. Some vocations seem more of a fit, and others less so. The im-
plied suggestion is to avoid the weaker areas and emphasize our reported
strengths. And so, as these profiles help us sort out the complexities of
our abilities and interests, they seek to narrow down the possibilities into
something manageable, something we can grasp and act on.

Some of the profiles give us a numeric scale of strengths vs weaknesses, while others provide a visual map or picture of our personality
pattern. It's an effective way to communicate the results of the testing.
Much of my life has played out within the boundaries set by those maps.
It feels safe inside the boundaries. Even comfortable.

But intuitively we know that there is much, much more to each one of us, more than a profile or map can ever show. My story is one of being called out of the boundaries of my personality profile map. I cannot say that it is painless, but it is liberating. And, of course, it requires faith.

Newspring began with a visual arts program for children and youth. My college major was economics, not art, and I am a retired CPA. Yet, despite the obvious misfit between this ministry and my background, the arts program has blossomed, helping at-risk students develop their skills, pointing to careers as visual artists, photographers, graphic designers, etc.

Almost immediately, people appeared who knew a lot about art. Others came forward to help build strong ties with the local schools. Needless to say, I had no idea of the red tape involved in building a program that interacts with public schools.

The key point here is that we built the program to fit the skills and aptitudes of the at-risk students, not the skills and aptitudes of the founders of Newspring. We saw the need and responded, and then our Lord provided what was needed to make it work.

All of this is to say that your personality profile map is good input for your thinking. But don't let it rule you because our Lord may have other ideas. He knows you from the inside. So if you are willing to march off the map of your personality profile into unknown territory, you can trust that He will be there to guide you.

1
YOU ARE NOT LIKELY

Go away from my window
Leave at Your own chosen speed
I'm not the one You want, Lord
I'm not the one You need.
It ain't me Lord, no, no, no it ain't me.

APOLOGIES TO BOB DYLAN

Lord, I am clearly not the one You want for this adventure.
In fact, I am the *least likely* person for You. I can name one hundred better
people, more qualified, stronger believers, even better looking.
Let me call them for You. I have their phone numbers right here!
Please forgive my hesitation. Amen.

And yet, I cannot resist You. I wish I could. You don't bully me into
following; You are far too subtle for that. No words are spoken. And
You don't come at me from above, below, front, or back. You come at me
from *inside*.

And that's the worst possible place, because that is where I am weak,
ugly, and failing. Where I can't really defend myself. Don't You see why
You should pass me by?

O Lord, you have searched me and known me.
You know when I sit down and when I rise up; you discern
my thoughts from far away.
You search out my path and my lying down,
and are acquainted with all my ways.
Even before a word is on my tongue, O Lord, you know it completely.
You hem me in, behind and before, and lay your hand upon me.
PSALM 139

So who am I? The unlikely one, the longshot. The shepherd boy called to be David, the warrior king. Esther, the reluctant queen called to save her people. The uneducated fishermen called to change the world. Saul, the persecutor, called to build the church he had fought to destroy.

Jonah tried to hide from His call. He couldn't. Moses made excuses. Our excuses won't work either. Neither can we hide.

We follow a God of the unlikely. The women who were the first to witness the Resurrection, how likely were they? The teenaged girl who carried the Lord in her womb? Listen to Mary:

Here am I, the servant of the Lord; let it be with me according to your word.
LUKE 1:38

The angel hadn't asked if she wanted this mission. It wasn't a job interview. Moses wasn't asked to take two steps forward to be on holy ground. He was already there.

God is not going to take no for an answer. Could these people have said no? Can you?

And the most unlikely one of all: the King who left glory beyond imagining, who came to live with us as a servant and to die a sacrificial death. Our God is a God of the unlikely!

2
IT'S NOT ABOUT YOU

Ray Kinsella: *"I did it all, I listened to the voices,
I did what they told me, and not once did I ask
what's in it for me."*
Shoeless Joe: *"What are you saying, Ray?"*
Ray: *"I'm saying ,. . . what's in it for me?"*

– FIELD OF DREAMS

Lord, I always begin with me. How do I feel? What must I do?
But why can't I begin with You? With who You are. With Your great love.
With Your calling on my life. Lord, help me to change
my point of reference from me to You. Amen.

How many times did Jesus say, "Not my will but yours"? But not me. So much of my life is spent building a résumé. It's expected. If I don't do it, someone else will build my résumé for me. And we know the difference between a great résumé and a mediocre one, don't we? You see, we are conditioned.

Most of us achievers find it difficult to ask for help. Most men won't even ask for directions!

Our culture tells us that it's all about us. Can you find comfort in the fact that in His Kingdom, it's *not* about us? We are not the initiator, we are the object. The object of what? Of His love, His leadership, His calling. He is our shepherd in all things, including the work He has called us to do.

Jesus told His disciples that they didn't choose Him, instead, He chose them. And so it is with you. You are chosen by Him for this work. But it's not about you, it's about Him. Can you deal with that?

So after what may amount to a lifetime of striving to look good, and doing it on your own terms, you've been called to a spiritual adventure, one that God Himself has ordained. Can you truly look to Him? Can you suspend your ambition? Can you suppress your desire to look good?

What does it look like to give your life over to God? To strive to build His résumé and not yours? To risk looking bad in the eyes of others while following His lead?

But we have this treasure in clay jars, so that it may be made clear that this extraordinary power belongs to God and does not come from us.
2 CORINTHIANS 4:7

There is no formula for keeping God at the center. As a mature Christian you understand the erosive nature of our culture, how it will subtly pull you away from the spiritual focus of your calling. Your part is to see the erosion and resist, not just for yourself but also for others.

So who are you? You are the one called to honor God in your work, to strive every day to keep Him at the center. You truly live in a clay jar. It's not impregnable. It's not all-powerful. It's not omniscient. It doesn't necessarily look good, and maybe it's even cracked a bit. But inside? There is a treasure there, placed there by God. And that treasure, united with God, can change the world.

If it's not about you then who is it about? It's about the one who called you and the one who guides you. It's about the one who lives within you, often imperceptibly, but who is always faithful and who loves you without measure.

For we are what He has made us, created in Christ Jesus for good works, which God prepared beforehand to be our way of life.
EPHESIANS 2:10

3
IT'S NOT ABOUT ABILITY

Lord, I have a five-year plan for my life, and believe me,
this work is not in it. I'm really not a very good fit for it.
You can see that can't You? You must know countless others
more qualified and even more interested than I am, others
who are better suited, whose résumés outshine my own.
Has there been some mistake? Why me? Amen.

It is hard to find any character from scripture who was well qualified. King Saul possibly came the closest. Wealthy, handsome, and tall, he just looked like a king! Yet Saul failed.

> *But the Lord said to Samuel, "Do not look on his appearance*
> *or on the height of his stature, because I have rejected him; for the*
> *Lord does not see as mortals see; they look on the outward*
> *appearance, but the Lord looks on the heart."*
> **1 SAMUEL 16:7**

Why did God choose Saul? Was it to show that even the best-looking résumé doesn't matter to God? By contrast, the messiah was foretold to appear very ordinary, with no pedigree and no obvious qualities of leadership. And John the Baptist? He was just plain weird. But Jesus said that no one in the Kingdom was greater than John.

Even Paul, who was educated and came from a prominent family, had to endure losing it all for the sake of Christ. He called the accomplishments of his previous life rubbish. He literally threw his résumé into the trash.

Consider your own call, brothers and sisters: not many of you were wise by human standards, not many were powerful, not many of noble birth. But God chose what is foolish in the world to shame the wise, God chose what is weak in the world to shame the strong; God chose what is low and despised in the world, things that are not, to reduce to nothing, things that are, so that no one might boast in the presence of God.
1 CORINTHIANS 1:26-29

Paul's words are perhaps even truer today. If anything, our culture values wealth, power, education, and especially appearance more highly than in the first century.

When we review scripture we come across figure after figure who seemed unfit for God's call, yet answered it, and, as a result, found abilities they'd never known before. Moses, the murderer, hiding out as a sheep herder, returns to Egypt to face Pharaoh. Gideon the farmer becomes Gideon the warrior/general. The disciples, who struggled throughout Jesus' entire ministry, finally become leaders after Pentecost. Mark, who deserted Paul, is later called back to be his trusted aide.

So what about you? You can despair over your lack of qualifications and preparation. But, in the end, perhaps your life's greatest opportunity to honor God is to accept His calling with humility and energy, knowing that any success is His, and knowing that the Living God is not just "living" in the abstract, in some distant place, unreachable by any human means. No, He is literally living in you, closer than your own breath!

It is our choices, Harry, that show what we truly are, far more than our abilities.
ALBUS DUMBLEDORE, HARRY POTTER AND THE CHAMBER OF SECRETS

4
YOUR REAL NAME

Lord, I have carved out a space for myself in this world.
It has boundaries that I can accept, and it is just the least painful place
that I can find to live. I realize that I've compromised things to live in this
space, and that some of those compromises have distanced me from You.
Sometimes I have wished for the courage to break out of my box,
but it's pretty comfortable here, living within myself.
Please forgive my lack of courage and believe that I am sorry
to ever keep myself from You. Amen.

Names don't mean much in our culture. Believe it or not, your parents actually thought that "Buffy" was a cute name for you. "Caitlyn" is beginning to fade: "Jonah" and "Chloe" are now popular but were seldom used a generation ago. Names come and they go.

On the other hand, Native American cultures gave great weight to names. Did you know that "Pocahontas" means "she is playful" in Algonquin? "Sacagawea" means "bird woman."

God also seems to take names more seriously than we do. He made a big deal of renaming Abram and Sarai as Abraham and Sarah. Jacob became Israel. Simon became Peter. Saul became Paul. James and John were nicknamed the "Sons of Thunder."

Much has been written about our false self. Actually it should be false selves, because each of us has many. In the world of the false self, Billy grows up to become William because it sounds more mature. We might not make an appointment to see "Doctor Susie," but "Doctor Susan" sounds better, and "Doctor S.B. Brown" sounds better still.

What are our false selves? They are the working definitions of ourselves that we build over time. Why do we need them? We need them because they work. They enable us to navigate through life, presenting an acceptable image to our families, to the workplace, to friends, and even at church. We learn to adjust our behavior, appearance, and even our names to fit the various environments in which we find ourselves. Judge Jones is "Daddy" at home and "Fred" on the golf course, but still "Freddie" to mom and dad. Some of us become very adept at changing masks and are successful, while others struggle and find themselves out of favor, never quite fitting the expectations of others.

But our false selves are only partially true: they are indeed working definitions, useful to meet the needs of our circumstances. The real question is: are they really us?

Each of us also has a true self which is the identity given to us by God. It's who we are on the inside, with all masks stripped away. The true self transcends all of the false selves we can create; but to many of us, the true self is an unknown figure, a shadow we little know.

God knows our true self better than we do. And He seeks to unite, not with our superficial false selves, but with our true self. What's more, He gives a name to our true self, a name that we will only know when all barriers between Him and us are finally exposed and dismantled. Until then we must live in tension between our many false selves and the true self that He cultivates. Perhaps the first thing we'll hear when we arrive in His Kingdom is our real name, the name He gave us at the foundation of all creation. I look forward to hearing my true name, my eternal name.

In the meantime, we are invited to step out of our box of compromise, out of the life of our false selves. Those whose false selves have been very successful find this especially hard.

Here's a way to look at yourself. It's called Johari's Window. It shows that you are more than the false selves that you show to others. You are more than the sum of your secrets, even more than the blind spots, qualities that others see in you and that you fail to see. God sees it all and much, much more than any human can see in you.

	Known to Others	Hidden from Others
Known to Self	False selves (working definitions)	Secret selves
Hidden from self	Blind spots	Known only to God

There is much to discover about your true self. Your calling to spiritual adventure can open you to a deeper understanding of who you really are if you are willing to place yourself in His hands. Your calling may not seem like a good fit for you, but trust our Lord, He knows better. He can reveal incredible things about your true self if you will let Him. But you must come out from behind your false selves and be vulnerable to His teaching. And, if you do, then maybe, just maybe you will hear Him whisper your true name.

5
WHAT IS YOUR REAL GIFT?

Lord, I often feel inadequate. Compared to others, what do You see in me?
I am limited, not very good at anything in particular. And I fear that it shows.
The question keeps coming back: Am I really called to this?
Did I hear it wrong? Is there some mistake? Are You punishing me for
something? Lord I read Your Word and take comfort, but only until the next
episode of inadequacy sweeps over me. I know that You call me to faith and
that You promise to walk with me. Forgive me for failing to remain confident
in your promises for more than a few minutes at a time. Amen.

---

*"I don't know who or what put the question. I don't know when it was put.
I don't even remember answering. But at some moment I did answer
Yes to Someone—or Something—and from that hour I was
certain that...my life, in self-surrender, had a goal."*
DAG HAMMARSKJOLD, FORMER SECRETARY-GENERAL
OF THE UNITED NATIONS

So what is your real gift? Are you gifted at all? Your modest, false self would assert that you are only slightly gifted (it's bad to toot your own horn). Your aggressive, false self would take on the attitude of a job interview, inflating every possible quality.

But what about your true self? Are you *really* gifted in any way? We've already established that you are an unlikely person called to a spiritual adventure. We've also established that while you live for the most part in a variety of false selves, God sees your true self. He sees qualities in you that you fail to see. He should: He put them there.

But as we have said, it's not about you anyway. You are to be used by Him, His instrument in a troubled world, in the lives of people starving for love.

So what is your true gift? It's simple. Your true gift, the place where God has equipped you so beautifully, is in the quality of your response to Him. You can do no better than to say "Yes!" to Him. If you don't know it, this ability to respond is a huge gift, one that only a very few ever act on.

Noah said yes and, until the waters rose, he looked like a fool. Esther said yes and risked her life. So did Rahab. Elijah did the same. John the Baptist died for saying yes, as did Jesus' disciples and Paul. Their résumés may not have impressed, but their willingness to say yes cannot be denied.

And, really, saying yes was all that was expected. But the answer had to be "yes" every day. A "yes" in the face of apprehension, fear and suffering. "Yes" even in the face of doubt and apparent failure.

By teaching "Do not judge" (Matthew 7:1), the great teachers are saying that you cannot start seeing or understanding anything if you start with "no." You have to start with a "yes" of basic acceptance, which means not too quickly labeling, analyzing, or categorizing things as in or out, good or bad, up or down. You have to leave the field open, a field in which God and grace can move. Ego leads with "no" whereas soul leads with "yes."

RICHARD ROHR

Can you say "yes" to God today? If so you are in very good company. And you are gifted!

"For the Son of God, Jesus Christ, whom we proclaimed among you, ...was not 'yes and no'; but in him it is always 'yes.' For in him every one of God's promises is a 'yes.'"

2 CORINTHIANS 1:19

6
ARE YOU A VISIONARY?

Lord, sometimes people compliment me as a visionary or as
someone who can build something from nothing. But, inside, I struggle
with that. Everything that I have done and built came from You.
All I did was say "yes" to Your leading. The compliments are nice,
but they make me feel uncomfortable. I try to witness to You as the true
visionary, but I usually express it inadequately. Amen.

A re you a visionary? A creator? A builder? Where do your gifts
intersect with God's purpose? Who gets the credit? Can you contend
with success? Can you even define success?

> *"...For I have not spoken on my own, but the Father who sent me has
> himself given me a commandment about what to say and what to speak.
> What I speak, therefore, I speak just as the Father has told me."*
> **JOHN 12:49-50**

You are more than a pawn on a chessboard, moving outside your own
volition. But you are also less than the initiator, the architect, the imple-
menter. It is a strange tension.

Among Jesus' disciples, Peter seemed to struggle the most with this
tension. He quickly descended from speaking great truth—"You are the
Messiah"—to speaking for Satan as he tried to co-opt God's plan by rein-
ing Jesus in: "This [the Crucifixion] must never happen to you!"

Your charge is to live in that tension. Every day. As a spiritual entrepreneur, called by God Himself, you will be looked to by many. You are a key face of your ministry and an integral part of it. You may even be in charge. But all followers of Christ must find the way to point to Him and reflect Him into their community, their stakeholders and clients.

So are you responsible or is He? Yes. Are you a founder? A leader? Do you point to Him as the true founder, the true leader? Yes. Do you know what success means? Do you allow Him to define success? Yes. Are you God's partner in His great work? No. You are a servant, a follower, a child of God. And more than that, you are His beloved.

You can do no more than look to Christ, the model and perfecter of our faith.

Some may call you a visionary, but there is one true vision, and it is the vision of the Father. We don't know when it will come to fruition. Even Jesus said He did not know when it would happen. But listen to the Father's ultimate vision:

"Then I saw a new heaven and a new earth; for the first heaven and
the first earth had passed away, and the sea was no more.
And I saw the holy city, the new Jerusalem, coming down out of heaven
from God, prepared as a bride adorned for her husband.
And I heard a loud voice from the throne saying, 'See, the home of
God is among mortals. He will dwell with them; they will be his people and
God himself will be with them; he will wipe every tear from their eyes.
Death will be no more; mourning and crying and pain will be no more,
for the first things will have passed away.'"

REVELATION 21:1-4

7
THE FINISH LINE

Lord, my ego wants me to be the complete leader and singlehandedly take
Your calling all the way to the finish line, to complete Your work.
I sometimes tell myself that I can really do it, that there is nothing beyond
my ability. But experience says otherwise. Forgive me for buying in
to my own foolishness, for acting as if I can do it all.
Forgive me for not looking to You, the completer and perfecter
of everything. Forgive me for blinding myself with my own ambition
for glory and for failing to witness to Yours. Amen.

So neither the one who plants and the one who waters is anything,
but only God who gives the growth.
1 CORINTHIANS 3:7

Moses didn't enter the Promised Land. David didn't build the temple.
Jesus' three-year ministry was abruptly terminated, leaving only
twelve apostles and just 120 followers. None of the churches started by
Paul existed for long. And yet, the thread from each of these continues,
following at times a tortuous path. God's plan continues to unfold. But it
unfolds in His way, at His pace, following His timing.

So where does that leave you? Can you let God finish your work?

I am confident of this, that the one who began a good work among you will
bring it to completion by the day of Jesus Christ.
PHILIPPIANS 1: 6

He doesn't promise to bring it to completion *through you,* and in fact He seldom does that.

Imagine what Jesus' prayer towards the end of His ministry might have been if He were here today:

> **Jesus:** Father, this just isn't going as well as I had hoped. These people really aren't as far along as I hoped they would be. And there aren't as many as I think we need.
>
> **God:** If I can multiply loaves and fishes, don't you think I can multiply disciples?
>
> **Jesus:** But Father, if I had more time, perhaps there would be a better foundation for the Church. Three years seems awfully short.
>
> **God:** Your job isn't to build the Church. I will use others for that, in generations to come. You are the Lamb, the Sacrifice, the Redeemer.
>
> **Jesus:** Well, some of these people are not too bright. I feel uncomfortable leaving the entire Plan in the hands of these knuckleheads.
>
> **God:** Yes, they are about as unlikely as you could ever find. I always call the unlikely. You know why? So that no one can boast. I am the root, you are the vine and they are the branches. They will bear fruit.

In the end, Jesus did complete His work. Not the work of building the Church, but the work of redemption. He alone could say, with confidence, to the Father: *"It is finished!"*

Can you accept the call to a spiritual adventure and let God finish your work?

Nothing that is worth doing can be achieved in a lifetime;
therefore we must be saved by hope.
REINHOLD NIEBUHR

8
PRODUCING RESULTS

Lord, I am trying so hard to produce something: to finish, to proudly display the fruit of my labor—a good result. Intellectually, I understand that only You define what "finished" really means, and only You define "good fruit." But I can't let go of my own definitions. And I prefer them to Your obscure agendas. My personal ambitions drive me in a very unforgiving way. Please forgive my lack of faith and deference to You. Amen.

...but test everything; hold fast to what is good...
1 THESSALONIANS 4:21

There are too many ways to go, too many possibilities for a spiritual entrepreneur like you. Opportunities present themselves on a daily basis. And there is no roadmap for the path ahead, showing which strategies to follow and which to avoid. As a spiritual entrepreneur, you are in a position to do nothing but test the opportunities that come your way. And then observe what God will do with them.

Boards want strategies and funders want results. And our egos drive us to want to comply, to produce *something,* to finish.

But you are called to be a foundation builder, and to let others finish. Paul tells us that he didn't wish to build on the foundation of another (Romans 15:20–21). He was a true spiritual entrepreneur.

Can you imagine if Paul had been required to produce a strategic plan for his missionary work? He plunged into uncharted waters, looking for any place that would offer what we might call "traction." He had little data to go on, and could not possibly project the costs and benefits of his journeys.

And imagine Paul's annual board meeting when he reported back the results: beatings, imprisonments, riots, and yes, a handful of believers in a handful of cities, most of whom would drift away from the faith or into heresy without correction from a scolding letter, a return visit by Paul or one of his faithful assistants. Read 2 Timothy chapter 4 to get a picture of what results Paul might have to report to his board of directors toward the end of his ministry. But even with all of Paul's discouragement, he could still say, "I have finished the race." How could he say that?

How? Because, amazingly, he had laid the foundation. Ultimately, Paul's work succeeded. Did Paul finish his work? Did he produce significant results? No, others took over for him. Like those mentioned in Hebrews chapter 11, he "died in faith without having received the promises" but saw them "from a distance."

So consider your own spiritual adventure. Can you be content to give yourself to something that you can't finish? To ultimately hand it over to another? To see it change from the original vision? To patiently wait on results? To see things you have tried and tested fail?

Paul did. And why? Because of the "unsurpassing value of knowing Jesus Christ." Allow the Father to produce results in His way, not yours.

9
LETTING GO

Lord, I must admit that I believe that no one can do this like I can.
After all, You called me to this, didn't You? You must have seen something
in me, right? But now we are some distance downstream and things are
becoming challenging. My fresh vision seems a bit worn out.
And I am tired. My patience with others is beginning to fray.
Why don't they know what I want? Why can't they see what I see?
Lord, are You going to fire me? Amen.

We see leaders who hold on to their positions far too long. Elected officials have term limits, and, in the minds of some, they can't be short enough. Corporations have boards that are sometimes astute enough to know when a leader is out of gas.

But just as often, we see leaders clinging to their position long past the time when they should have stepped aside. A feeling of ownership takes hold, and especially in the case of the founders, an organization can be so identified with them that it becomes detrimental to everyone. It leaves no space for anyone else.

Leadership should be seen as generational. The founder generation, which did all the groundwork, built an organization on a shoestring and did incredible things, may not be best suited as the organization matures.

As great as he was, Moses could not get the children of Israel into the Promised Land. Joshua arose to become the perfect second-generation leader. David was spinning out of control and lost his grip on his people, and it took Solomon to stabilize the kingdom.

What's more, the founder generation may come to an attitude of possessiveness that is not healthy. What was once new and fresh can become stale as an organization matures. Second-generation challenges and opportunities can go unaddressed as first-generation leaders continue to live in a first generation context, with first generation mental models.

There is a stickiness, a reluctance to let go. But letting go is necessary. Unfortunately, the longer it goes, the stickier it becomes as the first generation holds on ever more tightly.

There is no finishing. There is only transition. Wise founders will know when it is time to prepare for the second generation and will embrace the change.

Question: What if Jesus, after the resurrection, had stayed around and built the Church? Surely to the human mind, that would have been preferable to the collection of leaders He left behind. Jesus could surely have done a better job than Peter, John, Paul, and the others. Inquiring minds of the day would surely have wanted to know why He left so suddenly.

But that wasn't God's plan. He evidently wanted the Church to be built on faith and with the Holy Spirit as the encourager. So it may be with your founder generation.

According to the grace of God given to me, like a skilled master builder I laid a foundation, and someone else is building on it. Each builder must choose with care how to build on it.
1 CORINTHIANS 3:10

II.
ARE YOU
REALLY ALONE?

I t was amazing. Once I found myself starting Newspring, people began to appear, almost out of nowhere. They came to volunteer, to lead, and to contribute financially. They came to pray, to advise, and to open doors, connecting us with volunteers, partners, and donors.

Some stayed for only a season, while many others continue still. Most have become very close friends, with Christ as the binding agent. Without Him, the appeal of the new ministry would have soon worn off by the natural friction that plagues organizations as they grow. The newness fades and energy wanes.

But our spiritual focus has kept this ministry alive and vital; as a result, our volunteer retention is over 75% per year. The bonds that connect us have not so much been the I'll-serve-on-your-board-if-you'll-serve-on-mine bonds of mutuality. It goes much deeper. The relationships go deeper than those founded on the false charity of seeing your picture on the society page at the gala, or on guilt over the gap between rich and poor. They penetrate to the very bedrock of our shared faith in the community called into being by Christ Himself. No other foundation will work.

And it hasn't stopped. Faces continue to appear, as one new arrival brings several more, multiplying into a network of individuals, churches, foundations, and corporations who answer God's call. The miracle is that it's so easy to see God's hand in it, as we find almost daily surprises in those who answer His call.

Still, my path has been a lonely one at times. It has kindled in me a desire for the deepest possible relationships, for friends who will go the distance with me. He has given me an inner circle, and I am grateful.

The odd thing is that by nature, I don't easily make friends and am somewhat of a loner. Now, in this new entrepreneurial life, He has awakened a hunger in me for deep and transparent relationships with those who will walk the road with me. It's almost as if I cannot get enough of the spiritual intimacy that I once avoided.

I hope that you are at a place where you feel that hunger too. Feeling the hunger for deeper spiritual relationships is a good sign. Why? Because He planted that hunger deep inside you, and you have finally dug deep enough to uncover it. I hope that the thoughts that follow give you a feeling of unity with all spiritual entrepreneurs who walk what at times can be a very lonely road.

1
LEVERAGE

Lord, You place people all around me and I take it for granted.
Sometimes I don't even see them until they practically pound me over the
head. Often I reject them based on my criteria and not Yours.
Your record throughout scripture shows how Your grace can leverage the
people You've called to walk with me. Forgive me for giving it lip
service and always wanting more and more. Help me to look
to Your power and grace for everything. Amen.

O ur God is all about the few. The small. The one. He is seldom, if
ever, about the many, the army, the masses. Jesus claimed that He
could request "more than twelve legions of angels" to rescue Him, and the
Father would provide them. But that wasn't the plan.

His parables were about small things, including the tiny mustard
seed. About one coin, about one sheep, one pearl, one small amount of
leaven, one narrow gate. Why? To show the power of God. The widow's
one small coin in the offering plate outweighed the larger donations of
the wealthy.

Gideon raised a large army, but God cut it back to only 300 against the
powerful Midianites. God is all about leverage. And we are supposed to
leverage too. Not the power of man, but the power of God Himself. All it
takes is one spiritual entrepreneur. See what God can do with just one!

Consider the ministry of Jesus. He never had many followers: after three years, He only had 120. They came and went: first, John the
Baptist (briefly). Next, the twelve; only a few others are named: Mary
Magdalene, Jesus' mother and some others. This was not an impressive
group. A modern church-planter might have been fired after three years

with such a record. But it was enough. The Father's plan leveraged these followers in a surprising way and changed history.

Paul was given Barnabas and then lost him. Silas came next, and eventually Mark, who Paul had previously fired. Timothy, Titus and a few others who also came and went. There was no planning team, no follow-up team, no communications team, and no security team. But this spiritual entrepreneur and his team laid the foundation of the Church as we know it.

So what are we to do? How does God's leverage actually work in today's world?

Only live your life in a manner worthy of the Gospel of Christ, so that...
I will know that you (plural) are standing firm in one spirit, striving
side by side with one mind for the faith of the Gospel.
PHILIPPIANS 1:27-28

Accept the people who God recruits to help you. Don't expect an army. Don't expect what the world considers the "cream." Come together in a way that honors the God who called you, in one spirit, striving side by side with one mind. *Unity in Christ is critical to leverage.*

Your mission is important, and so is your vision. But even more important is your attention to who you are as part of a team of disciples. Continue to focus on your calling and on the one who called you. Continue to look to Him for His grace to lead you. Find tangible ways to put Him first, and He will not fail you.

2
PRAYER

Lord, I confess that prayer is the easiest thing for me to neglect.
It's not that I don't recognize prayer's importance. But distractions pull me
away in so many directions. And prayer seems to be such a passive activity.
It doesn't produce anything, at least not anything tangible or immediate.
So instead, I answer emails, develop grant proposals, meet with people,
and do any other thing that produces something that I can show to others
and to myself. And yet, I know that without prayer there would be no energy
and no spiritual vitality to what You've called me to do. I also know
that without prayer, including the prayer of others, I would quickly
lose any grounding that I have gained in You. Amen.

Devote yourselves to prayer, keeping alert in it with thanksgiving. At the
same time pray for us as well that God will open to us a door for the word.
COLOSSIANS 4:2, 3

Where does your energy come from? What keeps you going? When you suffer the inevitable dips and depressions, where do you go?

Prayer is your primary channel to the source of your spiritual adventure: your calling, your guidance, your sense of unity, your ability to love in the face of adversity. It is your most important resource. It's too bad we can't bottle or package it.

A spiritual entrepreneur must *work* at prayer. It's not easy. As Paul says, we must "devote" ourselves to it. We can't be lackadaisical and we must "keep alert" in prayer. Erosive forces, both internal and external, seek to pull you away, to unplug you from the Source. What's more, a spiritual entrepreneur must be a prayer leader, calling others into a community of prayer.

Any community lacking a foundation in prayer is like the house built on sand. It will not stand against the storm. Worse, it will find itself slowly and imperceptibly eroded away by the everyday tides of life. Your success as a spiritual entrepreneur depends on many things, not least of which is prayer. You find unity in prayer among your leaders, volunteers, donors, clients, etc. *Prayer is the one activity of your calling that links everyone involved.* It doesn't leave anyone out.

"When we work, we work; but when we pray, God works."
MAX LUCADO

This widely quoted truth surely assumes that we know that God is always working, whether we pray or not. Despite that, there is a quality to prayer that gets God's attention. It's not necessary to know how this works. Just remember that your personal prayer life, and the prayer life of those who support you are mystically bound together, creating a network that links our heavenly Father into the life of your calling, giving it an energy and a vitality that the world simply cannot give—or even explain.

3
PARTNERSHIPS

Lord, my natural inclination is to do it (i.e. pretty much everything) myself. And when I explain my vision to others, I am impatient if they don't immediately get it. I realize this is arrogance and is unwise. You continue to humble me through experience, but I am a slow learner. Teach me patience and the value that others bring to my calling. Amen.

Unfortunately, the church is not a good model for partnerships. Denominations divide and divide again. They have become competitive. Working across denominational lines is a rarity. Cooperation among neighboring churches seems a distant priority.

Scripture doesn't help much either. Jacob partnered with his uncle Laban, but Laban could not be trusted. Joseph partnered with the Egyptians, but that worked only while Joseph and Pharaoh still lived. Later, that partnership soured quite a bit. David partnered for a while with his enemies, the Philistines, but that also ended badly. Why didn't these partnerships work? They didn't work because they lacked any shared values.

But, there can be a great deal of leverage in partnerships, especially for a young organization trying to establish itself. And it's possible to do so without compromising your values. Even if you can't find an established partner who shares your exact mission and/or vision, you may find one whose mission/vision complements yours, and whose set of values is compatible with your own.

Are you all about education? Look to the local schools, community colleges, and universities. Healthcare? Look to hospitals, physician groups, and medical schools. Economic development? Look to local corporate partners, chambers of commerce, and universities.

And in everything, look to local churches and other faith-based organizations. A network of partners can be a powerful force in a community. You can be the catalyst that brings them together. Your investment in a network of partners can yield significant benefits, both to you and to the community you serve.

Partners can accelerate your growth by opening doors, enhancing your credibility, and serving as sources of volunteers and funding.

What's more, partners can become part of your mission field. Your mission, your vision, and especially your spiritual values will influence theirs in ways you could never predict. So as you begin to penetrate the community you serve, you will also begin to penetrate the hearts of your partners.

It may be tempting to bend or hide some of your foundational values in order to fit in with your partners. Don't yield to this temptation! Your organization may be the leaven needed to mobilize and energize your partners, the key ingredient in the masterpiece created by the Master Chef. Your mission, vision, and values may serve as the launching pad for an entire community!

4
YOUR INNER CIRCLE

Lord, I really long for close friends in this adventure. Walking the road alone is not only lonely, it's intimidating. I need navigators to help me stay on track and to share the experiences of this spiritual adventure. Only I want to have the right to reject anyone who You might choose for my inner circle. I am afraid that my criteria outweigh Yours, and I am sorry for that. That is not as it should be. Forgive me for not trusting You and for rejecting the unlikely people who You place in my unlikely path. Amen.

Prophets are not without honor, except in their
own country and in their own house.
MATTHEW 13:57

Where were Jesus' boyhood friends? They were not among the twelve, and not even mentioned as followers. We never hear even a single name of an "old friend" of Jesus. Why didn't He pick out any long-time friends to follow Him?

Did Paul the former Pharisee recruit any Pharisees to join him? If he tried, he must have failed. No, Paul's companions, his inner circle, came to him, sent by God. First, Barnabas, who was key to introducing Saul the Persecutor to the suspicious Christian community. Later Paul was joined by Silas, Timothy, and others. None were Pharisees, and most were locals in the early churches, like Priscilla and Aquila, who hosted a church in their home. Many were not even ethnic Jews.

Just as you are the unlikely person called by God to a spiritual adventure, so it will be with your inner circle. He will raise up people around you who may not fit your expected mold. They are meant not only to support you, but also to stretch you, disagree with you, and correct you. These friends in your inner circle serve as voices that you need to hear, even if the message wounds you.

And your long-time friends? Be careful. Your friends may not understand your calling, may wonder who this person is they thought they knew. They may even reject your calling, just as Jesus was rejected when He returned home to His friends in Nazareth.

So let the Father do the calling, and do not be too surprised at His choices. Embrace them.

What actually is your inner circle? It is not necessarily your board of directors or your executive committee. It's your closest traveling companions on your spiritual adventure. Your inner circle is made up of those few who are bonded together in truth and love. And the glue that bonds you together is more than a common mission and vision. The bonding agent is none other than the love of Christ, knitting hearts together in fellowship with Christ Himself at the center.

Fools think their own way is right, but the wise listen to advice.
PROVERBS 12:15

III.
RESULTS

To say that I was conditioned to make a god out of results would be an understatement. The world of public accounting/business consulting, where I spent twenty-eight years, is the seminary of metrics and outcomes measurement. In that world, the ultimate in performance was to be right all the time, and to produce ever more billable hours.

This competitive, metrics-driven environment was quite formative to those of us who stayed for a career. From the beginning, we were molded to a set of values driven by the reality of marketplace competition. But, down deep, I always resisted the notion that results and measurable outcomes should represent the pinnacle of worth. And I knew I could never be right all the time (just most of the time). Maybe it's the contrarian thinker in me, or maybe it's some other force at work, filing off the rough edges of black and white judgments based only on numbers, return on investment, and calculated risks.

There is no escaping the demand for results. Funders require them, volunteers draw energy from them, and observers make snap judgments based on them.

But I have to say that this new life as a spiritual entrepreneur has released me from worshipping at the altar of metrics. It's not that I no longer care about measureable results; it's more that I don't lose sleep over them anymore. I am more interested in people and relationships, which is quite a turnaround for someone conditioned to add up every column of numbers in sight.

That feeling of release has allowed me to be formed by a new force: the Holy Spirit. Now, the vitality of my ministry no longer comes from a feeling of accomplishing a goal or reaching a benchmark. The vitality comes from within, from the Christ within me, who gives me comfort, direction, and most of all, peace. And, of course, it also comes from the people we serve, one at a time.

I hope that you too will find release from the altar of anything that detracts from the one who has called, prepared, and equipped you to be a spiritual entrepreneur.

1
BIGGER ISN'T NECESSARILY BETTER

Lord, I confess that I want to look good. I have built multiple false selves just for that purpose. One of my false selves aims at looking like a strong, but compassionate, leader. I even have one false self that focuses on (false) modesty. Another one is the successful entrepreneur who can build a huge organization overnight. They really cover the map! But You teach me that bigger isn't necessarily better. Results come in all shapes and sizes, but I seem to prefer the big, showy ones. If You did not teach me how to look good, then I must have learned it elsewhere. Please forgive me for practicing it so much. Amen.

Jesus was not a preacher who, like some contemporary evangelists, converted thousands at a time. Nor was Paul. Many of those who Paul brought to Christ are actually mentioned by name in his letters. It was very likely one at a time or in small groups.

The book of Acts does not mention a single church growing too large for its meeting place, or struggling with the challenges of rapid growth.

But our egos want big, don't they? Big what? Big everything, except big problems. But in Jesus' terms, entrance to the Kingdom was available only through a narrow doorway or a gate to a sheepfold. His parables and metaphors never suggest anything big. When Jesus is "standing at the door knocking" He is standing at your front door—the door to your heart—not at the door to an auditorium or a stadium.

And yet, the societal problems we take on are, in fact, big ones. No one launches a faith-based organization to solve small, marginal, or peripheral needs.

Consider this: God's method seems to be to plant seeds that ultimately become movements. Jesus did that with the twelve and with the 120 followers mentioned in the book of Acts. Likewise, Paul started small churches that organically spawned more small churches. These outposts of the new Christian faith gathered enough momentum that by the time the first generation churches began to die out, a generation of new churches was poised to take their place. And on and on it has gone, more like a chain reaction than a single explosion.

So perhaps your challenge is to plant the seeds and let God give the growth. Will your ministry ever become large? Perhaps. But just as likely, it may serve to light a match to a problem or community need, combining with partners to create an impact far beyond the capacity of any single organization.

Or you may find yourself serving as a parent, giving birth to more spiritual entrepreneurs, whose second-generation organizations go far beyond yours. And so, these children of your adventure may do great things, creating a movement whose life and reach may go far beyond your imagining, and far beyond the life of your organization.

Remember, impact is a goal, not growth. Don't make "bigger" your primary goal.

One who builds a high threshold invites broken bones.
PROVERBS 17:19

2
WHO DEFINES SUCCESS?

Lord, it's true that I define success and failure. I simply can't switch
off my judgmental mind. And worse, my definition is greatly influenced
by the opinions of others. "People who count" and who influence me
not only include board members, donors, volunteers, etc.,
but also other spiritual entrepreneurs. I feel competitive with them.
But Your image of the "suffering servant" is chilling to my ego.
Please help me to align with Your definition and to tune out the spoken
and unspoken critiques and pressures of others. Amen.

Jesus emptied Himself and defined success in terms of obedience to the
one who sent Him.

Let the same mind be in you that was in Christ Jesus,
who though he was in the form of God, did not regard equality with
God as something to be exploited, but emptied himself...
PHILIPPIANS 2:5-6

There is nothing wrong with success. Your organization was formed,
not to fail, but to succeed. It meets a societal need: adding value, making
a contribution. And you can trust God's calling to your mission. Stay true
to it. Work hard at it.

But be careful how you define success. The Father will use you as He
pleases, for His purposes, which may not equate to your stated goals. He

may lead you through a wilderness for a while before you begin to see where He is taking you. Don't fight Him.

Think of the path that Joseph followed. Go back and read his story in Genesis. After his dreams of success (brothers bowing down to him), Joseph's life was hijacked and followed a path that included captivity, slavery and prison before he discovered God's definition of success. God was grooming Joseph to be an executive! Only then could Joseph understand that what his brothers had done with evil intention was meant by God for good.

There is nothing wrong with defining goals. Goals motivate and provide a benchmark for measuring progress. Likewise, it is important to track results in the best way you can. Reporting results provides important feedback to your organization.

But if you are not careful, goals and success can become your god. Pressure from internal and external sources, and their definition of success, can literally crush you. It is only your spiritual grounding, together with your inner circle, that can keep you on track, looking to God as the final arbiter of success. Ultimately, you are accountable only to Him.

How does God look at success? Perhaps the best definition can be found in the "fruits of the spirit" listed in Galatians: love, joy, peace, etc. These may be hard to translate into goals, and reporting on them may be close to impossible. Perhaps that is why Jesus never defined success for His disciples. He simply told them to persevere to the end.

...At all costs avoid one thing: success ...If you are too obsessed with success, you will forget to live. If you have learned only how to be a success, your life has probably been wasted.

THOMAS MERTON

3
MISTAKES

Lord, I am too afraid to make a mistake. And I know why. Mistakes are bad enough in themselves, but the real problem is that they make me look bad in the eyes of others. Help me to release my internal "mistake meter" and freely follow You wherever You lead me. Help me to learn from mistakes and grow from them. Help me to admit them, not only to myself, but also to others. And forgive me for hiding and rationalizing them. Amen.

The book *Mistakes of the Old and New Testaments* has never been written. It would be too long! Character after character messes up, beginning with Adam and Eve. In fact, the Bible is actually the story of human mistakes and the redemptive power of God.

I have not failed. I have just found 10,000 ways that won't work.
THOMAS EDISON

The true story of a mistake is not the mistake itself, but what happens next. What do you do about it? Do you allow it to defeat you? To paralyze you? Are you too focused on rationalizing it or blaming others? Or are you willing to let Christ guide you, teach you, lift you, and put you back on your feet? Can you be patient enough to understand the mistake?

To reach something good, it is useful to have gone astray.
TERESA OF ÁVILA

Let God speak to you through mistakes. How do you hear Him? First, take comfort from His Word, speaking to you from antiquity as you read story after story of His redemption of mistake-prone humans. This redemption story is, in fact, *the* story of scripture. After humankind had strayed, Christ came to show us the way to His Kingdom, and to make sure that we knew that, despite our mistakes, He desperately wants us to be with Him.

You also hear Him through your inner circle and through your own cognitive ability to learn from experience. That includes your prayer time, your interactions with key people and your life at the grassroots of your ministry. It's very difficult to learn from what's happening on the ground when you are at 50,000 feet. Watch and listen.

Finally, to the extent you can, you must suspend your ego and your need to look good. Remember, you are a pilgrim on a journey of spiritual adventure. It has risks and dangers. You were never promised a smooth, easy road. It is a road requiring patience, including patience with yourself and others.

So cut everyone some slack, including yourself. We follow a God who guides and leads us, but He shows us only the next step or two, not the entire journey. His finish line may be just around the corner. We travel in faith knowing that our ultimate destination is with Him!

I have come to know a God who ...recruits people like the adulterer David, the whiner Jeremiah, the traitor Peter, and the human-rights abuser Saul of Tarsus. I have come to know a God whose son made prodigals the heroes of his stories and the trophies of his ministry.

PHILIP YANCEY

4
GOD'S RESULTS

Lord, I confess that I have expectations: expectations that are shaped by culture, ego, peer pressure and personal experience. I recognize that Your expectations are dramatically different from mine. Forgive me for clinging to my own expectations and closing myself to Yours. Open my heart to see life as You see it, not as the world sees it. Amen.

E xpect the unexpected!
When you respond to God's call, there is absolutely no way to know what He has in mind. Scripture is rife with example after example of what humans would call unintended consequences.

Joseph never dreamed he'd end up living in Egypt, much less serving as the number two man in the country. Selection as queen was not on Esther's radar screen. We have no idea what the twelve disciples imagined when they joined up with Jesus. Experiencing tongues of fire dancing on their heads was probably not something they considered!

What do God's results look like? They look like love in action. They feel like a life unlike anything you may have ever felt. Stories begin to emerge: stories of transformation, of new energies, of healing, of people finding new life. And many of these stories come from unexpected places, not necessarily from those you originally set out to serve. They come from volunteers, even bystanders.

Those who cared for the "least of these" never dreamt that they were serving Christ Himself. Saul must have expected punishment when Christ knocked him off his horse and blinded him. What he got was something entirely different.

God's results are always exceptional: exceptional devotion, exceptional giving, exceptional depth of commitment, exceptional love and compassion, exceptional energy, exceptional grace. They are never mild or marginal or mediocre. God's results may be hard to explain, and you can spot them only if you are open to the unexpected. They feel like a life that is apart from your normal life, something "other" and special.

More than anything, God's results are personal. Statistics are great, but the true story of God's results comes in the form of changed lives, one at a time. We strain to anticipate results by looking straight ahead, to see what's coming. God's results never come from straight ahead, but instead, from around the corner. We simply can't see them coming.

And finally, God's results are part of His story of resurrection. In the final analysis, everything points to resurrection. And, as a spiritual entrepreneur, you are not only part of the story of the birth of a ministry, but you will also be part of many stories of resurrection.

For my thoughts are not your thoughts,
nor are your ways my ways, says the LORD.
ISAIAH 55:8

5
METRICS

Lord, I am conditioned to measure up and even excel. I can't remember any instance where You were competitive or where You counted up the results of Your work. But competition drives me, and that's not all bad— is it? I feel pushed to produce measureable results and to do so quickly in order to gain funding and support. Please forgive me for elevating metrics to a level equal to You. Amen.

Jesus was all about the individual: the woman at the well, the Gerasene demoniac, the cripple at the pool, the man lowered through the roof, etc. He did preach to crowds and He fed thousands but He died in the company of a few friends, soldiers, and mockers. Witnesses to His resurrection numbered no more than three.

But we live in the twenty-first century don't we? Volunteers and funders have many options and they demand metrics, i.e. quantitative results. Our outcomes had better look good, and they'd better be constantly improving. Otherwise we risk losing support.

Was Jesus against metrics? We don't know. But we do know what He was for: the prisoner, the sick, the poor, the "least of these." His disciples thought that interacting with children was a waste of Jesus' time. Poor time management! But over and over Jesus told us that the individual is of limitless value. He told us that the ultimate in love was to lay down one's life for a friend—not for a crowd.

The best we can say today is that Christ understands. He wants us to succeed. But if and when we make metrics into a god, we take our eye off of those who we were called to serve. And that crosses a line for Christ.

Christ lived and died for people—not for numbers, or for any quantitative measure of success.

What makes our challenge even tougher today is the demand for quick results. Supporters lose patience if positive outcomes take too long to materialize.

So in the early stages of the work you are called to do, look for signs of progress, even small ones. Measure them if you can. Break down hoped-for outcomes into small steps that can show a direction of improvement.

And most of all, look for the stories of individuals whose lives are impacted by your ministry. You can find out by asking them. Keep your eyes and ears open, and sensitize yourself to the odd place to look.

Putting a face on your service and its benefits may not outweigh the absence of metrics, but it will touch the hearts of people who understand your vision and who are inclined to respond to you. And it will also keep *your* heart in the right place, focused on the individual people you've been called to serve.

If I look at the masses I will never act; if I look at a single person I will.
MOTHER TERESA

6
WHOSE "VALUE PROPOSITION"?

Lord, we have a mission statement and a vision statement. They define what we do. But on a regular basis You produce fruit through our ministry that we do not expect. These are outcomes that fall outside our activities and efforts. Sometimes we have no idea where they come from. Are we faithfully following You? Should we change our mission statement (not sure what we'd change it to)? Am I so blind to Your direction that I just can't see where this is going? Amen.

A value proposition is basically an understanding of the inputs and outputs of an activity. We are willing to work toward a goal, expecting to achieve a good result. Investors expect a return. So do donors and volunteers. So does anyone who gives of himself in any way.

And so we define a value proposition for our ministry. It goes like this: we will invest time, money, political capital, and other resources to produce a desired outcome. Presumably, this outcome is beneficial for those we serve. It also produces satisfaction, which is not a by-product, for those who give and invest.

But our Father also has a value proposition. It can be found in John 3: 16: "For God so loved the world that he gave his only Son, so that all who believe in him may not perish but may have eternal life." And God's value proposition overrides yours and also the value proposition of everyone else who tries to follow Him. His is the over-arching value proposition.

That's why your ministry has so many unintended consequences. At least it does provided you remain faithful to His calling to put Him first in your mission. And those consequences can startle you as you realize that He is working in the hearts of your volunteers, donors and clients, typically without your knowledge, until you are surprised to see fruit that you did not expect.

He is allowing you to be the catalyst, the channel of His love into the hearts of individuals who will hear His message of salvation through your work. All of this happens, even though you didn't necessarily intend it or even notice it occurring.

So often, people will come to you with stories of transformation resulting from your ministry, and you will say to yourself, "But I didn't do that!" Of course you didn't, but then again, those stories would not have happened without you.

So what is really going on? While you are feeding the poor, educating children, assisting the homeless, or any of a thousand other activities, He is actively winning hearts to Christ. And He is showering His grace upon people connected to your ministry. It's almost imperceptible until you are confronted with a heart that has been touched by His grace. It's His value proposition, and you will hopefully welcome it and marvel at it! And witness to it.

7
MANAGING EXPECTATIONS

Lord, the expectations of others are all over the map! Pleasing them all seems impossible. And I don't really know what is realistic. Your expectations are important to me, but I honestly don't know what they are. Can You give me a hint? I want to please You, of course, but others cry louder. I feel jerked around, but I want to feel grounded in You. Amen.

But to what will I compare this generation? It is like children
sitting in the marketplace and calling to one another, "We played the flute
for you, and you did not dance; we wailed, and you did not mourn."
For John came neither eating nor drinking, and they say, "He has a demon";
and the Son of Man came eating and drinking, and they say,
"Look, a glutton and a drunkard, a friend of tax collectors and sinners."
MATTHEW 11:16–19

Jesus had problems with expectations too. He just didn't fit the image of others, including His own family and closest followers (Peter: "that [your crucifixion] will *never* happen to you!"). When Jesus washed the disciples' feet, they resisted at first. His action did not fit their expectations. Martha expected Jesus to scold Mary for listening to Him instead of helping with dinner, but he didn't. Those in the Jewish power structure clearly didn't expect Jesus to criticize them, but He did.

How do you manage expectations? Not just those of your board, volunteers, and funders, but even your own expectations? Can your purpose and your actions ever satisfy the expectations of others?

*People look at me like I should have been like Malcolm X
or Martin Luther King or Rosa Parks. I should have seen life like that
and stay out of trouble, and don't do this and don't do that.
But it's hard to live up to some people's expectations.*
RODNEY KING

The expectations of others *will* become a test of your faith. Can you remain faithful to your purpose, despite the expectations of others? Your best course is to admit to yourself that you cannot change the expectations of others. However, you can at least start on solid ground by announcing your purpose early, before the assumptions of others have time to take root.

The first recorded public words of Jesus in Luke chapter 4 clearly stated His purpose:

*"The Spirit of the Lord is upon me, because he has anointed me
to bring good news to the poor. He has sent me to proclaim release to
the captives and recovery of sight to the blind, to let the
oppressed go free, to proclaim the year of the Lord's favor."*

Your mission and vision statements will help you set expectations. Use them to clarify what you are about and where your organization is going. You might also consider a third foundational statement: a statement of "Who we are."

A "Who we are" statement gives your organization an opportunity to explain to any reader exactly who you are. It might begin with "We are followers of Christ, called to..." A statement like that is hard to misunderstand.

And what about your actions? Just as Jesus announced His purpose early in the gospels, He also quickly demonstrated His purpose through His actions: healing, eating with tax collectors, and associating with sinners.

In many ways, your actions speak even louder than your words. Make sure that others can see your purpose through your actions. Early and often. And then allow Him to manage the expectations of others.

Mission: Answers the question "How will this organization reach its vision?" A mission can change as circumstances change and as goals are met.

Vision: A description of a future state that serves as a goal for the organization. Vision statements typically do not change during the life of an organization.

Who We Are: Identifies who is involved in the organization, in terms of its most foundational attributes. This statement should not change over the life of the organization.

Mission

Vision

Who We Are

8
DON'T DO THIS FOR THE GLORY OF IT!

Lord, my motives are not pure. I am sure that You know it. Part of me wants to serve you simply for the joy of it. But part of me wants glory. I attempt to suppress this part, but it sometimes comes out and I fear that others see it. There is no escaping it. I am sorry for it and am so happy that in spite of my mixed motives, You do not abandon me and still use me. Amen.

The Gospels are filled with stories of Jesus' disciples saying the wrong thing at the wrong time. Often their faux pas related to "Who is the greatest among us?" or "Can we sit at your right hand in the kingdom?" These frequently came at the worst possible time—just after the transfiguration or when Jesus explained His sacrificial fate.

It may be enough to say that a mature person knows better than to strive for glory. After all, life does have a way of humbling us.

For over a thousand years, Roman conquerors returning from
the wars enjoyed the honor of a triumph—a tumultuous parade.
In the procession came trumpeters and musicians and strange animals
from the conquered territories, together with carts laden with treasure and
captured armaments. The conqueror rode in a triumphal chariot,
the dazed prisoners walking in chains before him. Sometimes his children,
robed in white, stood with him in the chariot, or rode the trace horses.
A slave stood behind the conqueror, holding a golden crown,
and whispering in his ear a warning: that all glory is fleeting.
PATTON (1970)

Jesus' commentary on glory seekers is that whatever praise they receive in this life is their reward.

But we are all human, aren't we? Some of the very qualities that have led us to this spiritual adventure have a dark side of ego and a desire for glory. Two sides of a coin cannot be separated, but one side can live in the light while the other remains in darkness. And the coin still has value despite its dark side.

The glory of God is a human being fully alive;
and to be alive consists in beholding God.
SAINT IRENAEUS 2ND CENTURY

Your glory in this spiritual adventure is to be with Him, to live in the faith that you have been called by Him and to see what He does as you walk the road together. There is no other glory in the world that can measure up to this.

Living with mixed motives is perhaps the price you pay for the privilege of this spiritual adventure. And, in the balance, it's not a big price compared to the wonder of His presence in your ministry. After all, it's the only way for a human being to be "fully alive."

Now to him who by the power at work within us is able
to accomplish abundantly far more than all we can ask or imagine,
to him be glory in the church and in Christ Jesus to
all generations, forever and ever. Amen.
EPHESIANS 3:20-21

9
WAITING FOR THANKS

Lord I know better than to expect or even to want thanks from You.
After all, I'm still in shock that You thought enough of me to choose me in
the first place. But I must confess that I do seek appreciation from others.
And when it doesn't come (and I never get enough), I simmer like a pot of
water about to boil. So I keep waiting to be thanked. Lord, forgive my
self-centeredness and help me to see through Your eyes. Amen.

Every one of my fans is so special to me.
JUSTIN BIEBER

Maybe you wish you had fans too. At some level we all want to be appreciated and perhaps we want even more than appreciation. But the thanks we deserve never come, or if they do, they are never enough.

But that perspective is backward. It is not our place to have adulating fans. We are not rock stars. Instead, as a spiritual entrepreneur, you must *be* a fan. A fan of whom? A fan of every volunteer who gives an hour to your ministry. A fan of every donor who gives a penny. And especially, you must be a fan of those whom you serve: the people who are struggling, who need encouragement and appreciation for their effort.

Consider the letters of Paul. Virtually without exception he begins with a word of thanks to the Father for those addressed in the letter. His letters don't fish for thanks from those he is writing. He is the *source* of thanks, the cheerleader for each new church community. And as a spiritual entrepreneur, *you too* are a cheerleader.

And that means finding ways to appreciate others—from your board chair down to the lowest or youngest stakeholder. Even when their contribution seems marginal to you.

Do you work with teachers? Healthcare staff? Church workers? Whoever it is, you must find ways to say "thank you" that are special to them. A simple note may be a start, but it's worth spending a little money to show your appreciation to special people. It's also worth throwing a party for volunteers, donors, and others who help you.

The hardest part is finding ways to appreciate these people, knowing all the while that they could have done more, given more and been more present to your ministry. It doesn't matter. They still need thanks, and those thanks must come from you and your fellow spiritual entrepreneurs. You can't delegate appreciation! And you can't measure the contribution of others against your own standard. If you do, no one will ever measure up, and no one will ever be thanked.

So don't worry about being thanked. In this lifetime you will never receive the thanks you deserve. Anyway, do you really want that?

Your reward will come. It may not be in this lifetime. Look at it as an investment account, where deposits are being made on your behalf. Later, you will wear your crown of glory and hear the Master say, "Well done, good and faithful servant, enter into the joy of your Master." Isn't that worth waiting for?

The world tells you many lies about who you are,
and you simply have to be realistic enough to remind yourself of this.
HENRI NOUWEN

IV.
WHAT SHOULD YOU EXPECT?

I had no idea what to expect when I started Newspring. It felt like I was being carried along on a swift-moving river with no time to consider possible outcomes. Perhaps that was made easier by the fact that it seemed impossible to imagine what success might look like. So I was gifted with a vacuum of expectations.

The expectations of others, however, were a different matter. They were all over the map, and what made it worse was the clamor for me to express lofty goals and grand strategies, to define success in a way that suited each person.

Disconnects appeared between founders and those who joined the first generation as leaders, volunteers, and donors. Questions of scope arose, of the pace of growth, and some even questioned the choice of communities to serve.

But our first year was anchored around statements of mission, vision and our "who we are" statement. Those defining concepts carried us, along with the determination of the founders, to stay the course.

Yes, some people fell away, and that was especially painful to me. I did not want to lose a single person. It still hurts, but I recognize it now as just one of the prices a founder pays: not everyone agrees with the approach, and many are impatient for unrealistically swift progress.

But I began to see a refining process taking place as we progressed. Those who stayed with the ministry began to come together in a community of shared values. And those values have consistently prevailed over arguments about scope and approach, and other specifics.

Chief among those values has been our spiritual foundation and the approach of relying on faith in Christ. Over and over we hear people say that is why they were drawn to our organization, and the reason that they stay committed to it.

Keeping those values in a place of importance has required considerable effort. I am sorry to say that, for us, it has not happened automatically but has required determination and perseverance. And so, as you read this chapter, my prayer for you is not for total unanimity. That is unrealistic. Instead, my prayer for you is for the patience, determination, and perseverance to keep your spiritual values as the guiding force for your ministry.

1
SPIRITUAL ATTACK

Lord, I never expected this to be easy. But some days I feel so lost, so low, so out of place. Voices tell me that I am not good enough to do this. Others whisper that no one else is good enough either. Inertia and negativity surround me. Am I being attacked? Is my faith really up to this? Amen.

So what will it be? From where will it come? You can pretend that you are immune to spiritual attack, that evil either doesn't exist or has already been defeated. But experience teaches otherwise.

Call it what you will: Satan, Evil, the enemy, or spiritual attack. Whatever you call it, you will experience it, and when it comes, you will know that it's real.

Spiritual attacks typically come from the inside, from the very heart of your ministry. They can look like many things: illness of a key person, betrayal of a close associate, internal rivalries, scandal, accusations, voices of criticism or negativity, and more. Our enemy draws from a rich arsenal of weapons.

What do you do? You can rejoice that your calling is sufficient to incite the forces of evil.

As they left the council, they rejoiced that they were considered worthy to suffer dishonor for the sake of the name.

ACTS 5:41

But do not rejoice too much! And do not welcome attack. Do not invite it.

For our struggle is not against enemies of blood and flesh, but against the rulers, against the authorities, against the cosmic powers of this present darkness, against the spiritual forces of evil in the heavenly places. Therefore take up the whole armor of God...
EPHESIANS 6:12-13

A mighty fortress is our God, a bulwark never failing;
Our helper he amid the flood of mortal ills prevailing;
For still our ancient foe doth seek to work us woe;
His craft and pow'r are great, and armed with cruel hate,
On earth is not his equal.
Did we in our own strength confide, our striving would be losing;
Were not the right Man on our side, the Man of God's own choosing;
Dost ask who that may be? Christ Jesus, it is He;
Lord Sabaoth, his name, from age to age the same,
And he must win the battle.

You are not expected to win the battle. We follow a God who calls us to be as wise as foxes, to know our own limitations. He is the one who is all-powerful, and He is the one who will win the battle. We are called to take up our cross and follow Him.

In my distress I called upon the Lord; to my God I cried for help.
From his temple he heard my voice, and my cry to him reached his ears.
PSALM 18:6

Our role in this spiritual adventure is to call on him when we are attacked. Give the battle to him. He and only He can prevail. He, and only He, is the source of our comfort and protection. He, and only He, can be our refuge in a time of trouble.

2
DRIFT

Lord, we are drifting away from You. I can feel it. The spiritual vitality that gave birth to this ministry is fading. As a result, the energy that ignited our mission is draining. Which is more important: our mission or our focus on You? It feels as if something precious is slipping through our fingers. And I don't know what to do about it, or how to combat the drift. I am sorry for my part in allowing this to happen. Amen.

We live in the real world, don't we? And that world is secular, with islands of Christ-followers in the midst of spiritual apathy, religious pretending, and even opposition. And just like the surf, those forces can erode your island of spiritual vitality that was so exciting at the beginning.

At worst we give lip service to God's presence, but then feel and act as if we were completely on our own. [Meetings] often begin with a sincere prayer, 'God be with us (as if God might be in attendance at another meeting) and guide our decisions and our actions.' Then comes 'Amen' and the door crashes shut on God-attentiveness. It is time to get down to business. Parker Palmer calls this 'functional atheism... the belief that ultimate responsibility for everything rests with me.'
GERALD MAY, THE DARK NIGHT OF THE SOUL

Several avenues offer hope to keep the spiritual fire burning:

- **Prayer:** the ultimate source of spiritual energy and discernment is prayer. It begins with you and your leadership team and your inner circle. If the prayer dimension of your ministry dies, the rest dies with it. *Prayer is the one activity that links everyone in your ministry, from the chairman of the board to the lowest and youngest person involved.*
- **Community:** we strengthen one another in community. Most important is communal prayer. Other activities, such as spiritual retreats, devotionals in meetings, communal worship, serve to keep the spiritual bonds strong.
- **"Who we are":** composing this foundational statement defines who you are in the most basic way, connecting you to the one who made you and who called you. It is a reminder.
- **Partnerships:** maintain partnerships, not only with other organizations who share common or complementary missions, but also with purely spiritual organizations (like churches, seminaries, prayer ministries, etc.) who can pray for you, provide spiritual programming for you, and connect with your stakeholders in spiritually supportive ways.
- **Renewal:** work with local churches to arrange renewal activities for stakeholders. These might include retreat weekends, such as Walk to Emmaus, Cursillo, and others.

Therefore, my brothers and sisters, whom I love and long for,
my joy and crown, stand firm in the Lord in this way, my beloved.
PHILIPPIANS 4:1

Stay alert to the damage that comes from drift. It can subtly undermine and disempower your ministry. "Stand firm in the Lord."

3
OPPOSITION

Lord, I view any opposition as a spiritual attack. Disagreements threaten me.
I want everyone to buy into my vision, my views, and my judgments.
Even any discussion of alternatives (other than mine) sours my stomach.
Forgive me for believing too much in my own judgment,
my own opinions, and decisions. Open my heart to others and
especially to You. Help me to listen better. Amen.

The basic question is this: How do you keep opposition constructive and healthy?

At a conceptual level, it's easy to concede that differing points of view yield better solutions and direction. The input of the many is generally better than the input of the few. But it's hard. Look no further than Congress to see an example of dysfunctional opposition.

Opposition doesn't have to be dysfunctional. But when individuals come to believe that their opposing thoughts and opinions are not valued by leadership, they can quickly shut down. Likewise, when principles are placed ahead of people, opposition will polarize an organization. Consensus is lost, sometimes irreparably. Loss of support soon follows.

Consider the councils of the early church as found in the Book of Acts (chapters 11 and 15). These heated discussions centered on what was to be considered orthodox Christian doctrine and practice. Leadership was informal, with no official hierarchy. Plus there was no defined procedure for making rules, no canon, and no institutionalized policies. It was all being made up as they went along.

And yet decisions were made, setting the precedent for further meetings as the tenets of the new faith were worked out. What can be learned from these meetings?

First, discussion was grounded on a foundation of core values. These were Christ-followers, who all had a stake in this new faith, and who all were passionate about it. Without a common grounding in core values (in our vernacular, "who we are" and "mission"), there would be no hope of any constructive conversation.

Second, they addressed the issues as soon as it was possible to meet. Postponing the conversation until later would have allowed different opinions to become entrenched, allowing egos to leap to competing positions. To the extent allowed by the transportation of the day, they got to these issues quickly, before factions could build.

Third, they respected and listened to one another, especially to the stories of Peter, Barnabas, and Paul as they described how they had witnessed the powerful acts of God. As the speakers related what they had seen and heard, the listeners came together in one mind and voice. They opened their hearts and minds to the leading of the Spirit of Christ.

A long dispute means that both parties are wrong.
VOLTAIRE

Finally, prayer is an advantage found only in groups centered on faith. Discussions that are saturated with prayer may produce disagreements, but they will inevitably occur in an atmosphere of grace and not contempt. That grace is a gift from our Father who dispenses it in abundance to all who honor him, even as they disagree. Without it, there is only arguing.

For he is our peace; in his flesh he has made both groups into one and has broken down the dividing wall, that is, the hostility between us.
EPHESIANS 2:14

4
OTHER PEOPLE'S DREAMS

Lord, You called me to start something, and I did. My vision (okay, Your vision) has propelled this ministry so far. Should I listen to the visions and dreams of others? Do they speak for You or just for themselves? My pride comes into play as I view them suspiciously, as if their thoughts and ideas were somehow heretical. Please forgive my pride and help me to open myself to the dreams of others. Amen.

You may say I'm a dreamer, but I'm not the only one.
I hope someday you'll join us. And the world will live as one.

JOHN LENNON

No, you are not the only dreamer.

The early church followed a path as an offshoot of Judaism. It did, that is, until Saul became Paul and went off to Antioch with Barnabas. Do you remember what triggered this deviation from the accepted path? It wasn't a strategic plan, it was something totally unexpected: persecution. It was persecution that scattered the faithful outside of Jewish territory.

And so they took their faith with them into an entirely new mission field, the territory of the Gentiles. Some protected their newfound faith, keeping to the small Jewish communities where they landed. But a few had other dreams, dreams of a faith that was for everyone, even those outside the Jewish tradition. Remember Peter's dream?

What was happening? The dreams of the Father were bigger than one person could hold, bigger even than one group could hold. So they were expressed through the lives and ministries of many. With some struggle, the wisdom of the fathers prevailed to open the faith to those once considered unclean and inferior. *The dam of exclusivity can never hold back the flood of the Spirit.*

Your ministry is no different. As a spiritual entrepreneur you must understand that God planted seeds in the hearts of others beside yourself. And those seeds must grow in their own expression of the Father's dreams, not just of those He planted in you. Remember, others will need to come along to complete your work.

Think of it this way: if the dreams of others did *not* materialize or were somehow crushed, your ministry would start and end with you and others of the first generation. It could go no further than the range of your own dreams, ideas, and abilities. The Father has much, much more in store. He cannot and will not be limited by you, or by anyone.

Now to him who by the power at work within us is able to accomplish abundantly far more than all we can ask or imagine, to him be the glory in the church and in Christ Jesus to all generations, forever and ever.
EPHESIANS 3:20-21

5
WATCH OUT FOR "EXPERTS"

Lord, I rely too much on my own discernment and judgment.
But looking to You only leads to ambiguity and doubt. It's hard to hold onto
my faith when I am so confused by choices, overcome with data and puzzled
by the directives of "experts." But You continue to call me to faith, and to
believe that this ministry truly is in Your hands. Please forgive me
for listening to so many voices other than Yours. Please forgive me for
listening too much to my own voice. And help me to tune in
to You so that your whisper becomes a roar. Amen.

*Always listen to experts. They'll tell you what can't
be done, and why. Then do it.*
ROBERT A. HEINLEIN, *TIME ENOUGH FOR LOVE*

So which is it? Are experts good or bad? There is always much to learn and always someone who can teach you. Should you listen?

Old Testament kings were advised by prophets, though they seldom listened. Moses listened to the wise advice of his father-in-law, who told Moses that he would go crazy without a better system of management. Moses listened, and thus the consulting industry was born.

The first century Jewish leaders were advised by one of their own, Gamaliel, and they found his advice helpful (see Acts chapter 5). They learned that it was futile to fight against God.

Experts are fine, but remember one thing: We follow a God who has always defied experts, mystifying the wise and elevating the uneducated and "foolish" of the world. In fact, God's record is spotless; He has never lost any battle between the wise and the foolish.

For the message about the cross is foolishness to those who are perishing, but to us who are being saved it is the power of God. For it is written,

I will destroy the wisdom of the wise, and the discernment of the discerning I will thwart.

Where is the one who is wise? Where is the scribe? Where is the debater of this age? Has not God made foolish the wisdom of the world? For since, in the wisdom of God, the world did not know God through wisdom, God decided, through the foolishness of our proclamation, to save those who believe. For Jews demand signs and Greeks desire wisdom, but we proclaim Christ crucified, a stumbling block to Jews and foolishness to Gentiles, but to those who are the called, both Jews and Greeks, Christ the power of God and the wisdom of God. For God's foolishness is wiser than human wisdom, and God's weakness is stronger than human strength.

1 CORINTHIANS 1:18-25

Nothing would be more fatal than for the Government of States to get in the hands of experts. Expert knowledge is limited knowledge, and the unlimited ignorance of the plain man who knows where it hurts is a safer guide than any rigorous direction of a specialized character.

WINSTON CHURCHILL

6
THE PERSON WHO GETS UNDER YOUR SKIN

Lord, I don't know why, but some people in this ministry really
know how to push my buttons. Within minutes of beginning a conversation
with them I am uptight and frustrated. Visions of harmony and teamwork are
swept away as my temperature approaches the boiling point.
How should I respond? Please forgive my poor interpersonal skills
and my unwillingness to forgive and go the extra mile. Amen.

*When we're dealing with the people in our family—no matter how
annoying or gross they may be, no matter how self-inflicted their suffering
may appear, no matter how afflicted they are with ignorance, prejudice
or nose hairs—we give from the deepest parts of ourselves.*

ANNE LAMOTT

Who put these people in my path? Why must I put up with them? Isn't this hard enough without these irritating people? If there is no one like this in your life right now, just wait. Your calling doesn't provide many ironclad guarantees, but if there are any, this is clearly one. Just hope that it's only one person at a time who drives you crazy and not an entire team! So go ahead and shake your fist at heaven if that makes you feel any better.

*The problem with people who have no vices is that generally you can be
pretty sure they're going to have some pretty annoying virtues.*

ELIZABETH TAYLOR

But remember: if we are blindly focused on getting things done, *any* obstacle—human or otherwise—becomes much more than a simple irritant. After all, voices of evil constantly whisper to us that obstacles must be overcome, if necessary, by any means possible.

If we take the irritations and annoyances personally, then their power over us leaps off the charts. Then we are giving this person *carte* blanche to *really* get inside our heads. But we really don't want anyone else living inside our heads except our Lord, especially not our annoying, friend.

God's agenda is much broader and goes much deeper than our own. His agenda includes softening a few hearts, yours as well as others'. Are we going to fight His agenda and cling to ours? Or are we going to follow His lead and practice grace and mercy? Will we go the extra mile with the person who forces us out on the road? Will we give the brazen borrower our cloak as well as our coat? Will we practice patience?

Much of the irritation comes from our own opinions of right and wrong. Richard Rohr calls that "dualistic thinking" and encourages us to practice "both/and" thinking. Those who disagree with us are not necessarily wrong. Multiple points of view may be valid.

When we stop judging those we see as obstacles as wrong or bad, we can see them in a new light, as people who have something to offer, something worth listening to. Sometimes, perhaps in very few cases, these irritating, annoying people who stand in our way can actually teach us something. And in *very* rare cases, we can actually learn to love them.

Next time a resentment, negativity or irritation comes into your mind...
and you want to play it out or attach to it, move that thought
or person literally into your heart space, because such
commentaries are almost entirely lodged in your head.
RICHARD ROHR, IMMORTAL DIAMOND

Jesus tells us to lead by being last, by humbly serving. It becomes very difficult to extend an antagonistic relationship with a person whose feet you are washing.

V.
QUALITIES TO
LEARN & USE

Starting a Christ-centered ministry is more like a marathon than a sprint. It's not just the idea of pacing, but rather it's the way you carry yourself through a long and sometimes grueling run. Keep your posture straight and you will avoid muscle cramps and back pain. Breathe correctly and you will conserve energy. Stop for bathroom breaks when needed. Don't press.

Some runners will pass you early on, only to fade later. Don't let the competition trouble you. Even be prepared to stop and help a competitor who has pulled a muscle. You are connected to the other runners.

Don't wear too much clothing because your body temperature will rise during the run. If you've overdone your outfit, be prepared to strip some of it off and leave it along the way. Don't neglect to wear good running shoes. Never scrimp on your shoes! The course may be rocky in places.

The hills on the course are especially tough, but everyone must run them. The downhill is as tough as the uphill because running downhill strains your ankles and knees. Don't run too fast downhill, or you might trip and hurt yourself.

Most importantly, stay on the path. Which path? The path that has been given to you. You won't be able to see the finish line for quite some time, so get comfortable with the progress you are making. If you need to set milestone points, go ahead and gauge your progress.

My Newspring race is not yet over. I will continue to run until His whisper changes, until He pulls me off the course. He is my coach in all things.

Most of the time, it feels like I have found a rhythm in my running. It is a life rhythm, not just a Newspring rhythm. It incorporates Newspring, my life in Christ, my family, church, everything. In the end, He desires all to become one.

Sometimes, I get out of sync and my rhythm fails. I try to be sensitive to His pace and have found that listening in prayer is the only way to re-calibrate myself to Him. I am imperfect at doing this. Often, He brings new people alongside me to get me back into His rhythm.

My prayer for you is to live without external pressures. Those inside of us are enough! Also to allow Him to relieve you of any voices that tell you that you can't do it, you're not good enough, and that you must go it alone. All of the qualities in this chapter come from Him, and all we need to do is to tap into them. They may not naturally fit your particular personality pattern. So like a marathon runner, if you want to avoid dehydration, you must drink *before* you feel thirsty. God's water will fuel you for the race ahead.

1
PERSEVERANCE

Lord, I must admit that this is harder than I imagined. The dreaming and visioning were easy and fun. But now I am grinding. Some days it feels like I am trying to run against a strong current in deep water. Some days feel like I am hitting a dead end. I try to take the longer view and surely can see progress. But it's never fast or strong enough. My conditioning to instant gratification clouds my vision. Please forgive my impatience. Amen.

The words "persevere" and "endure" appear in scripture over seventy times. This seems to be a primary theme in the Word. And there is more: Paul tells us in 1 Corinthians 13 that Love "bears all things, believes all things, hopes all things, endures all things." Is there a better definition of perseverance?

It's hard, though, isn't it? It's especially hard when you find yourself on a lonely road. So rely on the spiritual leverage of your inner circle and on your partnerships. And get close to the grass roots of your ministry. See the faces of those you serve. Touch them and be touched by them. Living only at the committee or board level can suck every drop of vitality from your ministry.

A committee is a cul-de-sac into which ideas are lured and then quietly strangled.
SIR BARNETT COCKS

Most of all, refresh yourself spiritually. Once the spiritual energy drains away, every task becomes an unwanted chore, every goal seems hollow and pointless, and the fellowship of your companions loses all vitality. There's simply no discernable love, no heart in it.

And it's not just you. As a leader, your job is to help others to persevere. You can pick them up. You can encourage them when they are down. You can be the face and voice of Christ to them. In reality, this is your highest calling.

Don't worry about the tangibles: the metrics, the reports, the actuals vs the budget. Build on the *int*angibles: the love, the witness, the fellowship in community, and the resurrection stories. Persevere in these things, and let the road take you forward in faith.

The Road goes ever on and on down from the door where it began.
Now far ahead the Road has gone, and I must follow, if I can,
pursuing it with eager feet, until it joins some larger way where many
paths and errands meet. And whither then? I cannot say.
J.R.R. TOLKIEN, THE HOBBIT

Ours is not the wider, easy path, but the narrow way. And when we persevere, we can take comfort in Christ, the one who walks with us, taking His cross and carrying it alongside ours.

But the one who endures to the end will be saved.
MATTHEW 24:13

2
LISTENING

Lord, I fear that I am listening to the wrong people, including (and especially) myself. I try to listen to You but, frankly, I don't really know how. And the voices that I do hear are so loud! They clamor for my attention. It's all so confusing. I really want to listen to You, but I just don't know how to quiet the other voices. Please forgive me. Amen.

It's too much. You can't listen to all the voices that assault you. We live in a world of constant and overwhelming communications. And it's not just verbal: there are so many books and seminars and inspirational speakers, too many to digest. It's too much!

So how do we sort it all out? How do we make sense of it? Is it possible to hear the "still, small voice" of God amidst the din? How do we avoid the dulling effect of the constant flood of noise from all the self-appointed experts?

For this people's heart has grown dull, and their ears are hard of hearing, and they have shut their eyes; so that they might not look with their eyes, and listen with their ears, and understand with their heart and turn—and I would heal them.
MATTHEW 13:15

Begin with the Word. Read it, absorb it, soak it up. Approach the Word, not like a textbook, but like a living thing, ready to breathe itself into your heart. Inhale it. Allow the Word to live in you. Listen with your heart, not your mind.

Then pray. Prayer is so multi-dimensional. So you pray for your needs, especially for those of your ministry. But, in addition, leave ample time to listen as you pray. Listen in silence. Be patient. God is pleased when we wait on Him. Wait on the Lord in your prayer time. Don't expect immediate answers.

Finally, do these things in faith: not necessarily faith in instant gratification, which poisons our culture, but believing in the "assurance of things hoped for and the conviction of things unseen." Believe that God listens and wants you to listen for Him. Practice listening.

I'm 36 years old, I love my family, I love baseball,
and I'm about to become a farmer. But until I heard the voice,
I'd never done a crazy thing in my whole life.
RAY KINSELLA IN *FIELD OF DREAMS*

From where will God's voice come? A cornfield? When will you hear it? Will it be a real voice?

Possibly, but we follow a God who uses many channels, mostly beyond our five senses. An otherworldly God will use otherworldly means of reaching out to us. In truth, we follow a God who resides within us, and who speaks to us from the *inside.*

So position yourself to listen for God as He speaks from the outside, through His word and through the unlikely people He places in your path (often through the *most* unlikely). But don't neglect to position yourself to listen for Him from the *inside* as well, as you feel that extra-sensory whisper that you simply can't describe in human terms.

3
FOCUS ON MISSION

Lord, You have called me to a mission and all the textbooks say that
I must focus like a laser on it. Yet You have also called me to a relational
ministry with children of Yours whose needs extend far beyond my stated
mission. I see those needs and feel them in my heart. Sometimes I can
call on others to help, but not always. So I seem to yo-yo
back and forth, wishing I could do more, but taking care not to over extend.
In the process, I often stir up a lot of dust, confusing practically
everyone, especially those who fail to see what I see.
Please forgive my confusion and indecision. Amen.

It's true, you can't do it all; you can't solve every problem. Leveraging to others can help. And partnerships are a great vehicle for leverage. Your network of organizations, churches, businesses, and even public entities can expand and deepen your reach into the community you serve. Cultivate them and appreciate them. And make it a point to understand not only the big picture of the needs in the community, but also the mosaic of organizations that serve it. Pull back the covers and look deeply into the corners; educate yourself about the "causal factors" and the ways partners might work together. Work to educate partners on the breadth and depth of needs in your community. Be a connector.

Accept that bringing in partners will never be enough. The nature of your calling is to an ever deeper, ever wider need. Why? Because at the bottom of it all, yours is a calling to love, to follow Christ into a sacrificial love for His children in need. Your stated mission is only one of many paths, merely the present path, to the community you serve. If you faithfully follow that path, doors *will* open to deeper callings. That's how God works.

> King Henry II: *Are you mad? You're Chancellor of England; you're mine!*
> Thomas à Becket: *I am also the Archbishop, and you have*
> *introduced me to deeper obligations.*
> *Becket*

Sticking to your mission will never be clean or easy. Love isn't limited to only one thing; it honors no boundaries of scope, distance or even time: it is boundless, eternal. And you are an agent of God's love in the lives of many, even some you may never meet.

You see, at the end of the day, you can't let Christ go forward without you. Because He will forge ahead, continuing to love those you serve in every way possible. He will go farther and deeper and wider than you can possibly go. Christ beckons you to follow Him as best you can, using the resources He has given you. That's why it's so important for you to see through Christ's eyes, *all* of the suffering, not just the part you serve. And it's also why it's so important to connect all those who serve to that bigger picture.

So manage your budget, your volunteers, and your staff. Keep to your mission as best you can. But *free your heart* to engage in "deeper obligations." The love of Christ is a deep current, reaching into every corner of creation, and its energy powers both you and your ministry. It will not be muffled, marginalized, or denied. It cannot be scoped or focused to fit any specific mission statement. So, to be sure, honor your mission. But at the same time, remember that you are called to respond to His.

> *I shall take up the miter and the golden cope again, and the*
> *great silver cross, and I shall go back and fight in the place and with the*
> *weapons it has pleased you to give me. It has pleased you to make me*
> *Archbishop and to set me, like a solitary pawn, face to face with the King,*
> *upon the chessboard. I shall go back to my place, humbly, and let*
> *the world accuse me of pride, so that I may do what I believe is*
> *my life's work. For the rest, your will be done.*
> **BECKET**

4
THE RIGHT TIME

Lord, I am conditioned to want it now. I mostly ignore Paul's definition
of love (1 Corinthians 13), which places patience as the very first attribute.
My will places success and achievement (mine not Yours) in first place,
above any other priority. Truly, I don't want to wait for anything.
I make excuses that it's all for You, hurrying to do Your will, but that is false.
I do it for myself. And in the process I run over people, ignore needs
and put You in second place. Please forgive me. Amen.

For everything there is a season, and a time for every matter under heaven.
ECCLESIASTES 3:1

When a new auto comes on the market, some will immediately check it out and buy it, while others wait to see how it performs and sells. Some will wait in line to be the first to see the new film while others will wait for the reviews.

By the time your ministry begins operations, you may have already logged several years getting organized, raising startup funds, building a board and developing plans and budgets. But aside from your closest friends (inner circle) and family, few others will know your ministry even exists. Some may even be shocked to learn of all the foundational work you've done, while others may never consider your long hours getting ready to launch.

Be sensitive to the timing of others. Some funders want a proven track record before contributing. Wait until they are ready to give. Likewise, some prospective volunteers, including close friends, may take their time checking you out. Respect their personalities (probably far different from yours) and their other priorities. Your best volunteers may need to disengage from other activities before joining you. You cannot expect them to simply drop what they are doing to help you or contribute to your ministry.

Give others the time and space to catch up with you. Respect their learning curve. Be patient. Remember, not everyone works at the pace of a spiritual entrepreneur like you. Not everyone is so excited about spiritual adventures, even yours.

Consider Jesus. He truly started a movement that has swept the world. And some of His followers *did* literally drop what they were doing to join Him. But only a handful. And remember Jesus' comment when His disciples tried to push Him into confrontation with the religious authorities? He kept saying that His time had "not yet come."

Jesus left all the timing to the Father. Even when He pleaded to "let this cup pass," the Father insisted that the timing was right. And as Jesus submitted to the timing of the Father, so are we called to do the same. God controls the clock.

5
STEPPING INTO A VACUUM

Lord, I don't really know what You want me to do. I mean, how am I to lead?
What does "leading" even mean? The bank account hasn't been reconciled.
We need copies of the agenda for our board meeting. And a room in our
office needs paint. Am I supposed to do these things? I occupy a box on
the organization chart and also have a job description, but it's only two
paragraphs long. It doesn't begin to describe all of the things that
I must do to keep this ministry going. I'm frustrated, and I feel like
a failure because I can't manage others to do the daily tasks and fight
the daily fires. Please forgive my self-absorption. Amen.

Remember, if your gift wasn't to say "yes" you wouldn't be in this mess!
Your spiritual adventure does *not* run like a well-oiled machine. And
in an embryonic organization, you can delegate only so much to others.
As a result, vacuums exist where tasks must be done and there is simply
no one available to do them. Who will step into the vacuum? Who will
perform the unwanted chore that simply won't go away?

Then I heard the voice of the Lord saying, 'Whom shall I send and
who will go for us?' And I said, 'Here am I; send me!'
ISAIAH 6:8

Spreadsheets are needed for a meeting. Thank you notes must be written to donors. Supplies must be purchased. Vehicles must be washed.
Procedures must be documented. Minutes must be taken at meetings.

None of this sounds like the leadership you read about in textbooks. And none of it is in your job description (if you even have one).

You can wait until the right person comes along to do these tasks. But you're not good at waiting. Or you can delegate and leverage all you can; still, there will always be more to do.

But remember your gifts as a spiritual entrepreneur, someone who is called to a spiritual adventure. Your primary gift is to simply say "yes" to the claim that God has put on your life. And when you said "yes" you said it not just to the tasks that excite you or please you or make you look important—or that fit your job description. Instead, you agreed to *all* of it, to whatever it takes to answer God's calling.

One of Jesus' final acts was to give us a vivid picture of true leadership as He stepped into a vacuum. He took a towel, wrapped it around his waist and washed the disciples' feet. One of them could have done it, but they were too proud. It was beneath them. So their Master lowered Himself to a servant's position, telling them that to lead meant to serve, to put others first. To step into any vacuum.

And so it will be with you. Your example of servant leadership, of stepping into any vacuum, any situation where others will not go, will be a powerful testimony to the love of Christ, our Master, who would step into the most difficult possible vacuum, the vacuum of the Redeemer, the Lamb of God. No one before or since has done or could do what our Lord has done for us.

The miracle is not that we do this work, but that we are happy to do it.
MOTHER TERESA

6
REST

Lord, I know how to rest. Sleep is (usually) not a problem, and I take days off from time to time. But rest in You is different, something entirely foreign to me. You promise a kind of rest that I yearn for with all my heart. It's a rest where I can lay down this weight that is crushing me. But rest in You eludes me. You promise a peace that passes all understanding, but I seldom achieve it. Is it all up to me? If so, what am I doing wrong? Do I need to stand on my head? Close my eyes and hold my breath? Please forgive my futility. Amen.

Thou hast made us for Thyself, O Lord, and our heart is restless until it finds its rest in Thee.

AUGUSTINE OF HIPPO

There is no truer rest than rest in the Lord. It's the deep, refreshing rest that our hearts long for. Before beginning your spiritual adventure, a good night's sleep might have seemed enough for you. But now, it's not enough. It will never be enough again.

Your spiritual adventure is not so much physically or mentally taxing. In fact, in some ways it can actually invigorate our physical batteries. But there must be a different battery somewhere inside of us that runs down in the absence of rest in the Lord. It drains especially fast in the throes of our spiritual adventure. So while we may feel physically and mentally charged up, the meter is running on our spiritual battery. And this spiritual battery is what ultimately gives vitality and meaning, not only to our spiritual adventure, but also to our very existence.

So what kind of rest do we need? Nothing short of the presence of our Lord. Nothing else will do, nothing will satisfy us, nothing will give us any relief from spiritual attacks, from spiritual lethargy, from drift, and even heresy.

Prayer is the medium chosen by God to channel His rest to us. In contemplative prayer, we can be the receiver, opening ourselves in total vulnerability to the Healer who can bind our wounds, restore our sight and drive away our demons.

Listening in solitude is the portal to the special rest that comes only from our Lord. Find your own place, your own time, your own context. Carve it out of your busyness and give it ample time. Make it a part of every day. It will feed you.

The ideal position from which to receive the Lord's rest is a kneeling position. When kneeling, we know that nothing is asked or expected of us. God's perfect rest can come to us as if down a one-way street. In humble silence, we can receive His rest unfettered by the distraction of conscious thought. Words will get in the way of this flow of the Spirit. Be still and know that He is God.

Prayer is not asking. Prayer is putting oneself in the hands of God,
at his disposition, and listening to his voice in the depth of our hearts.
MOTHER TERESA

7
GIVE GOD SOME SPACE

Lord, yes, I am a Type-A, driven person. Many forces drive me, not just one.
A desire for success is one of the most powerful. Or maybe it's a fear of
failure. As a result, I worry that your definition of success will foreclose mine.
Your goal is love and redemption, and I realize that my success and
Your love may not always be in step. So I try to lock You out when
my goals feel threatened. Please forgive my insistence on my way
and help me to let my personal ambitions die. Amen.

S o how do we peacefully coexist with God? How does His claim on our
lives and His calling fit with our personal goals and ambitions? How
do we submit to Him? How do we give Him the space He needs? How
does it feel to let Him lead?

...For it is God who is at work in you, enabling you both
to will and to work for his good pleasure.
PHILIPPIANS 2:13

We cannot give Christ only token space in our ministry. He must be the
center of it, not just a figurehead who is trotted out for opening prayers
and special occasions. It's not enough to open a meeting with a prayer and
then ask Christ to wait outside while we dive into our strategic plan. But
how do we keep Christ at the center of it all? How do we yield our personal
ambitions and opinions to Him? How do we give Him space?

Space for God in ministry is not possible without space for God in your personal life. You simply cannot skip over your own relationship with Christ while attempting to lead others in a Christ-centered ministry. Merely asking Him to bless your personal plans is not the answer.

There is no prescription for this. Opportunities for spiritual disciplines abound. But, at their core, faith is required. We must open our hearts and allow the Father to know us and to prune us. It can be painful. Ultimately we must believe, as Paul told the Philippians, that God is truly active inside us, not just for His work, but also to actually *shape our wills* to His perfect will. We must do it His way, not our way.

We must also carve out space in terms of time and attention. In Calcutta, Mother Teresa's sisters began and ended each day with hours of prayer. Prayer time could, of course, be shortened or even skipped altogether, providing more time for serving the poor. But that would be false efficiency. Spiritual energy would be lost and the very foundation of the mission would be jeopardized, ultimately leading to drift and failure.

Likewise it is with you. Failing to place Christ at the center will subject you and your ministry to our erosive culture that leads to personal drift and stagnation. Give your time and priority over to Him and be ready to see Him act in a powerful way, breathing energy into every day.

The good news of the Gospel is that He never tires of knocking on your door, never gives up on you. He works from the inside, helping you to allow those things that do not conform to the life He offers to die. He feeds you with His very life!

---

*So Jesus said to them, "Very truly, I tell you, unless you eat the
flesh of the Son of Man and drink his blood, you have no life in you.
Those who eat my flesh and drink my blood have eternal life, and I will raise
them up on the last day; for my flesh is true food and my blood is true drink.
Those who eat my flesh and drink my blood abide in me, and I in them.
Just as the living Father sent me, and I live because of the Father,
so whoever eats me will live because of me.*

JOHN 6:53-57

8
SPIRITUAL LEADERSHIP

Lord, I am not a pastor. This ministry needs spiritual leadership,
and I feel very unqualified to provide it. I'm pretty good at multi-tasking
but spiritual leadership is something that goes beyond my capability.
Yet I feel called to lead. How do I integrate spiritual things with my leadership
of this ministry? Maybe I'm too dense to see what You have in mind.
If so, please forgive my lack of faith and vision. Amen.

Where do you find spiritual leadership? What sources of spiritual leadership should you consider? Do you need an ordained pastor? And anyway, what does leadership look like in a Christ-centered organization like yours? Can leadership be compartmentalized? Is there a secular part and a spiritual part?

We are not human beings having a spiritual experience.
We are spiritual beings having a human experience.
PIERRE TEILHARD DE CHARDIN

We are called to live our faith, not to compartmentalize it. As a leader, you are called to lead from a spiritual platform, not a secular one. And as you bring Christ into the center of your personal life, so you must allow Him into the center of your ministry. That means offering your personal witness to what God is doing in your life and in the life of your ministry. It means that, as a leader, you also must provide a platform for others to offer their witness.

Providing the needed spiritual leadership is God's work, not yours. Give Him the space to do it. Your job is to follow His lead, to step through the doors He opens, to witness to what He does in your ministry. You must lead at a personal level, one person at a time. You must lead by following. In effect, you must be the chief follower.

Pay attention to what happens as doors open into the community where you serve. Cultivate the network of churches in the area. If there is no network, start one. Pay attention to what God is doing in the lives of those touched by your ministry.

Select board members and key volunteers with their spiritual stories in mind. Be ready to be surprised by those stories, from these sources as well as from those you serve. Be open to what God is doing in the lives of those you touch. You will be amazed at the stories, and you will also be amazed at how He uses you in the lives of others. You may not be a pastor, but nonetheless God will use you, to connect others to the springs of life found only in Christ.

But you are a chosen race, a royal priesthood, a holy nation,
God's own people, in order that you may proclaim the mighty acts of him
who called you out of darkness into his marvelous light.
1 PETER 2:9

Give God the space to work. Don't over-manage or over-engineer. He can, and will, perform miracles! Be a witness to His power and love. You will be amazed at what He does. Give Him the glory. *That* is true spiritual leadership!

It is no use walking anywhere to preach unless
our walking is our preaching.
ST. FRANCIS OF ASSISI

9
COMPROMISE

Lord, I want to be right all the time. Sometimes I truly believe that
I actually am right, if not all the time, then most of the time. That means the
thoughts and opinions of others must not count for much unless they agree
with mine. I realize that's a dangerous attitude and that I am asking for
trouble. I don't deal well with dissension and disagreement. Please forgive
my arrogance and the insecurity that is at the root of it. Amen.

You can be a lightning rod; not necessarily because you want to,
but because you hold on to your sense of being right, and because
of the fear of loss if you're proven wrong. Others will react in one of two
ways: some will take you on, challenging you openly or covertly, while
others will simply drift away, disengaging from what might have been a
fruitful ministry.

As a leader, did Jesus compromise? He certainly held to principles
of right and wrong, and He had no taste for hypocrisy. On the other
hand, He associated with sinners and did not judge others as inherently
bad or wrong. Among a testy group of disciples He was a peacemaker, a
shepherd. He proclaimed a leadership of humility, and backed it up with
action. There was, and is, no compromise in His love.

Paul and Barnabas eventually had a falling out, and there is no record
of their reconciliation. Paul and Peter certainly had their differences too.
In fact, Paul seems to have argued with pretty much everyone He en-
countered. His letters testify to His sense of what was right and wrong.
His writings include no admission of ever being wrong.

Yet, like Jesus, Paul also served as a shepherd to his flock. Most of his letters end with words of love and caring for brothers and sisters in the new churches. His letter to the Philippians concludes with a request for two arguing women to make peace.

Let your speech always be gracious, seasoned with salt,
so that you may know how you ought to answer everyone.
COLOSSIANS 4:6

A reading of Paul's letters quickly reveals that his words were not always so gracious (perhaps tough love?). Even so, his advice to the Colossians should be heeded. You may not always be able to compromise, to find common ground with differing opinions. But you can still seek to be gracious, to love and support others—even those who are adverse to you.

I therefore...beg you to lead a life worthy of the calling to which
you have been called, with all humility and gentleness, with patience,
bearing with one another in love, making every effort to maintain
the unity of the Spirit in the bond of peace.
EPHESIANS 4:1-3

As a leader of a Christ-centered ministry, you are called to do more than seek compromise. Your role is to be an example of grace and love. Others will take their cue from you. The rockier the road, the harder you must work to smoothe it.

Some leaders build a platform of power and in Jesus' words, "lord it over" their followers. Your platform must be Christ Himself, powered by the Holy Spirit, who will provide the faith, wisdom, love, and humility that you need to be a shepherd to those traveling with you.

10
VISION

Lord, we have a vision, and it's a good one. Volunteers are motivated by it and so are funders. I believe that it can serve us for a long time. But something is missing from it, and I'm not sure what to do about it. You see, our vision makes no reference to You. It feels like we've crafted a boat that will take us to the far shore, but without taking account of the water that lifts us or the current that carries us. Please forgive my omission. Amen.

The vision for your organization, whatever it may be, is legitimate. It must be simple and clear enough so that even a casual reading of it will capture attention. If not totally fixed and permanent, it should be enduring beyond the short term.

But God has a vision too. His vision may encompass yours, but it will inevitably go deeper and farther. God's vision unfolds at multiple levels. And, at its heart, God's vision is a story of redemption and resurrection, the rescue of one lost sheep.

Vision is the ability to see God's presence, to perceive God's power, to focus on God's plan in spite of the obstacles.
CHARLES R. SWINDOLL

As a spiritual entrepreneur, you have two roles: first, you are the articulator of your corporate vision. It will find its way into speeches, brochures, your website, etc. Your grant proposals and brochures will highlight it. Even your tax return will include your vision.

But God's vision must also reside in your ministry. As obscure as God's vision may seem, your second role is to become its translator. You (and others) will serve as the means through which God's vision is brought to life from the deep places of the heart into words and actions. In short, you must endorse and live out His vision for your spiritual adventure.

The two visions are not mutually exclusive, but they serve different purposes. Your corporate vision is meant to inspire volunteers and funders to achieve a future state that is beneficial. That future state can be measured in terms of outcomes and metrics.

God's spiritual vision is not so much about measureable outcomes, but instead it's a picture of a journey, an invitation to become a pilgrim, traveling His road, following Him toward *His* outcomes, most of which are beyond our imagining.

Charles Swindoll's quote above might be best altered a bit by changing "in spite of the obstacles" to "in the midst of the obstacles." You see, the obstacles and setbacks you encounter will likely become the primary stage on which God's vision plays out. How you react and deal with them provides the best opportunity to communicate to others what God is really about: the reconciliation of the world to Himself, one person at a time.

Your role in God's vision opens you up to significant misunderstandings on the part of others. Followers may find it hard to see the deeper purpose in your words and actions. They may see your emphasis on Christ as a waste of time in the face of so much to do. You may be called to account by boards, funders and other voices of authority. All you can do is trust what Jesus told His disciples: to let the Spirit give you the words to say when the time is right.

11
YOUR "OTHER" LIFE

Lord, what about my family? My friends? My church? I fear that I am neglecting them. Some of them see what I am doing and support it. Others probably resent my immersion in this spiritual adventure. Those who helped me get this started are getting tired. They didn't bargain for it to go on forever and I wonder sometimes if I'm running out of friends. Is there a balance somewhere? If so I haven't found it. Please forgive me if I have offended anyone, especially You. Amen.

Yes, there is life outside your ministry. You know it intellectually, but living it day by day is another matter. So many things come up, both challenges and opportunities. And they seem like tasks that only you can handle. Or so you think.

But is it really true that it's all up to you? Aren't you surrounded by some pretty capable people? And aren't new people attracted to your mission every day? And haven't those people been called by God Himself?

The verb "delegate" may be alien to your thinking. But if your ministry is to survive its first generation, you must build a pipeline of leadership. Otherwise, your personal energy and ability will be the limiting factors.

Thinking about this, your mind may wander to scriptural references such as "sell all you have and follow me" and "let the dead bury themselves and follow me" and "lay down your life." All of these suggest a total commitment, with no boundaries, no relief, and no rest.

All true but also consider the commissioning of the twelve to go and preach, as well as the commissioning of the seventy to do the same. Consider the Great Commission and Paul's use of his apprentices.

Delegation and an eye to a pipeline of leadership are just as scripturally sound as the passages about total individual commitment.

Also consider Jesus' social life with Mary, Martha, and Lazarus, as well as His times of rest. Jesus was undoubtedly 100% committed to His mission. But beyond that, He rested, enjoyed friends, and allowed His heavenly Father to feed Him through prayer.

How do we sort out all of this? Is our Lord asking us for a total commitment of time and energy, non-stop 24/7? Or is He asking instead for a total commitment of our hearts, to love without measure, to be ready to respond to Him and His direction?

The Lord is my shepherd, I shall not want. He makes me lie down in green pastures;
he leads me beside still waters; he restores my soul.
He leads me in right paths for his name's sake.
PSALM 23:1-2

Our Lord wants to feed you. And He knows just what is needed to restore your soul. As you allow Him to lead you in your ministry, allow Him to also lead you in your rest and relaxation. Allow him to lead you as you play, as you care for your family, and in every aspect of your life. Don't leave Him out of anything. He is the Lord of all!

12
RELATIONSHIPS

Lord, I am confused about relationships. I tend to see them now in
a very polar way. Some of my long-time friends haven't joined me in this
spiritual adventure. Others who did are now drifting away. And I harbor
negative feelings toward them as a result. On the plus side, those who are
attracted to this ministry have become new friends. But it's as if a
line has been drawn in the sand, dividing my relationships in a way
that I fear is not part of Your plan. Please forgive me. Amen.

The Gospels are filled with stories of encounters with Jesus. Many sought Him out with requests for healing various ills (a few even thanked Him). In other cases He took the initiative, as He did when He called the twelve.

There was never a quid pro quo with Jesus. He placed no demands on those He healed, never requiring a commitment or response of any sort. His healing miracles were never a strategy for recruiting or fund raising.

And likewise, Jesus offered no value proposition to those called to follow Him. There was no contract and no explicit reward offered. In fact, when some asked for a reward (sitting on His right or left in His kingdom), Jesus took pains to explain the suffering that was in store for them.

And so it must be with you in your spiritual adventure. Just as Jesus did not force any expectations on others, so must you allow others to follow their own path, even if it leads them away from you. If your ministry doesn't excite them, let them go. If they follow for a while and then drift away, do not condemn them for it. Binding others to your expectations, explicit or not, will mire you in disappointment.

Celebrate the new relationships that God gives you. They are among His greatest gifts. Give thanks for them and freely accept them with no strings attached. Consider the patience of Jesus with those closest to Him. He put up with their failures and shortcomings. He did not desert them, even when they couldn't stay awake with Him for even one hour while He prayed. He did not condemn them.

Allow God to navigate relationships for you. There will always be surprises, both from those who disappoint, and also in those who amaze and delight you. Never close the door on anyone, but give God the space and the time to work. Don't allow loyalty to the mission to divide your relationships into two camps.

Consider Paul and Mark. Early on, Paul essentially fired Mark. Loyalty was the issue. But God brought Mark back into Paul's life later, and Mark became a valued companion.

And what about loyalty? Can you imagine the loyalty shown by Jesus as He washed the feet of His betrayer?

13
BREAKING SOME EGGS

Lord, why aren't others willing to try new things? Or if unwilling,
to at least back off and allow me? Some of my closest supporters seem
so hesitant, so bound to convention and tradition. And I am not good with
that. My patience is thin; I expect others to keep up. When they don't,
I devalue them in ways that they probably see. Please forgive me
for hurting anyone, and for my impatience. Amen.

Jesus was certainly a new concept. Only a few could wrap their minds around Him, despite all the prophecies. The Incarnate Word. The Lamb of God. The Prince of Peace. He was the new wine, and the old wineskins simply couldn't hold Jesus. Not within their rules, power structures, or traditions.

Likewise, the new church reached across religious, cultural, and even ethnic lines as Gentiles embraced a faith that many Jews rejected. Quite a few eggs were broken in the process. Our God is an egg-breaker!

> *You CAN make an omelet without breaking eggs.*
> *It's just a really bad omelet.*
> **STEVEN COLBERT**

And so it comes to you. Perhaps your spiritual adventure is just one big experiment, with no roadmap, no blueprint, and little more than a bold new idea. But even if not, just the smallest step, safest change, or new path might seem momentous to some. There is a tolerance for change in all of us; more in some than in others.

Some fear that breaking an egg will lead to failure. Be charitable to them, for they cannot see. They have a risk-averse hold on their eggs, not realizing what's inside, and so never taste the hidden treasure.

Paul's nemesis, the circumcision party, could never leave the comfort of their egg. Contrary to Paul's guidance, they insisted that new Christians must also follow the rules and traditions of Judaism. But Paul pressed on and so must you. So break your eggs. Just don't be surprised when others react negatively. Breaking eggs has led to persecution, not only in biblical times, but throughout history. Especially within the church.

And that is where faith comes in. Faith is required for an egg-breaker. It is the conviction of what you cannot see, the assurance that breaking the egg will produce what is hoped for.

Only by faith did Noah build the ark. Only by faith did Abraham and Sarah begin their journey to a promised land. Only by faith did Moses face Pharaoh.

Rely on Him to lead you. There simply is no other way when you are traveling a new path.

"You don't really suppose, do you, that all your adventures and escapes were managed by mere luck, just for your sole benefit? You are a very fine person, Mr. Baggins, and I am very fond of you; but you are only quite a little fellow in a wide world after all!" "Thank goodness!" said Bilbo laughing, and handed him the tobacco-jar.
J.R.R. TOLKIEN, THE HOBBIT

14
HOW TO SAY NO

Lord, I am not good at this. Saying "yes" is a gift from You and I find it easy. But saying "no" is something else entirely. You must not have given me that gift. I realize that from time to time it will be necessary, and I also realize that there is an art to it. Mostly, it's a lack of courage, and a fear of rejection that get in my way. I understand that saying "yes" when I should say "no" can lead to trouble for everyone. Please forgive me. Amen.

In your role as spiritual entrepreneur, you will be invited to spend your personal capital on many things, some of them quite odd. A few will be easy to dismiss but others will be on the fringes of your mission and core values. Can you say "no?" Where do you draw the line? And how do you say "no" when the requests come from friends and supporters?

The art of leadership is saying no, not saying yes. It is very easy to say yes.
TONY BLAIR

Begin with the truth that there will always be more: more invitations, more opportunities, more requests—more than you can handle and more than you can delegate. When you say "yes" to a marginal opportunity, something else will need to be rejected or deferred. Even with all the leverage that comes from a spiritual adventure, your day is still just twenty-four hours long.

Learn to say "no" to the good so you can say "yes" to the best.
JOHN MAXWELL.

If this is hard for you, work at it! Practice is the key. Not to say that you should reject every request just for the sake of practice. But understand this: faith may be exercised as much by saying "no" as by saying "yes."

Saying "no" in love is part of your Christian witness. Jesus had to tell His disciples that it wasn't for Him to allow them to sit at His right or left hand in His kingdom. He told Martha that He would not enlist Mary's help for her in the kitchen. He gave these answers in clear but loving terms. And Jesus didn't waffle. He never put people off, saying, "Let me get back to you later." He did it with respect for the person He was turning down.

Oh, Jesus, what a trial it is to deal with so many opinions!
TERESA OF AVILA.

Watch others who are good at saying "no." It is an art that may not come naturally for an entrepreneur like you. Decide for yourself that telling the truth in love, painful as it might be, is preferable to offering an ambiguous "maybe."

Don't leave people hanging, waiting for a straight answer from you. Stringing others along, inviting hope that your answer might be "yes" when all along you mean "no" will serve to do nothing more than create distrust and disappointment. Likewise, ambiguous answers can lead to misunderstandings and hard feelings.

Above all, my beloved, do not swear, either by heaven or by earth
or by any other oath, but let your "Yes" be yes and your "No"
be no, so that you may not fall under condemnation.
JAMES 5:11-13

VI.
HOW DOES IT
REALLY WORK?

We started Newspring without a long-range (strategic) plan. We still don't have one, at least not a formal one. Plans are certainly not a bad thing; not that is, unless you place more faith in the plan than in our Lord, the one who called you.

To those of us who founded Newspring, operating without a plan meant two things. First, it meant that we had to be really good at learning as we went. We learned from mistakes and certainly found it advantageous to avoid repeating them. Equally important, we learned from successes too. As our art program grew and began to thrive, we took its model and expanded it to cover a wider population. It's much bigger now. We survey our stakeholders at least once a year and have learned a lot from their comments.

We also capitalized on the amazing miracles that appeared to literally shower down around us. Mostly they came in the form of people who seemed to materialize before our very eyes and offer to help, to contribute, to lead, or to connect. These miracle people haven't stopped coming. We have worked very hard to make them feel appreciated.

Finally, we continued to focus on our spiritual foundation and on the people, including those we serve as well as those who volunteer and contribute. It's easy to get confused between achieving a lofty goal and working relationally with people in the trenches. If you feel forced to choose between achieving a goal and building relationships with our Lord and with people, you need to consider very carefully why you are doing this in the first place.

A common comment from people associated with Newspring goes something like this: *"I never knew this population, its needs, or its potential until Newspring helped me put a face on it. Now I understand why you do this."* There is no substitute for putting a face on your ministry.

As educated people in a western culture, we tend to emphasize too much the destination, while the whole time our Lord is calling us to a journey. Choose the journey over the destination.

Focus on some of the practical elements of your calling. It truly is a journey, and I pray you can let our Lord guide you toward whatever destination He has in mind.

1
GENERATIONAL LEADERSHIP

Lord, the time is coming when leadership must be passed on.
Those of us who founded this ministry can feel it. New ideas and
opportunities pull at us, and distant doors are beginning to beckon.
But I am not a quitter. How do I stay faithful to Your calling when I feel
stirred to move on? And can I trust that it is Your will to pass leadership
on to others? Please forgive my confusion and lack of faith that
You know best and will do what is needed. Amen.

A twenty-first-century evangelist would certainly have done things differently from Jesus. Consider this: Jesus left no formal organizational structure, no documented strategy or tactical plan. No successor was anointed to lead in His place. He didn't even leave a will.

Despite all of that, Jesus created a *pipeline of leadership* that continues unbroken to this day. Much of His time and energy were spent with a small cluster of uncredentialed followers. They were apprentices, really. And absent any stated criteria for selection, these handpicked few became the second generation leaders of the movement we now call "Christianity."

Then Moses summoned Joshua and said to him in the sight of all Israel:
"Be strong and bold, for you are the one who will go with this people into the
land that the Lord has sworn to their ancestors to give them; and you will
put them in possession of it. It is the Lord who goes before you. He will be
with you; he will not fail or forsake you. Do not fear or be dismayed."

DEUTERONOMY 31:7-8

Scripture bursts with other stories of leadership transition. David to Solomon. Elijah to Elisha. Paul to Timothy. What can we learn from these examples?

First, the pipeline must be relational. It requires a *significant personal investment* from the first generation to the second. No example can be found in scripture of second-generation leaders simply stepping into their new role. Significant mentoring was always required. Read 2 Timothy to get a full picture of leadership being passed on.

It's also important to note that the pipeline must be started *well before* any planned transition. Jesus invested three years in relationship with His followers. Likewise, Paul traveled with Timothy, Titus, Silas, and others long before passing on the mantle to them.

A *deep faith* is also required: not just faith in the new team but faith in the Spirit who will guide them. You can impart only so much information, direction, and guidance before moving on. It will never be enough. Jesus relied on the Spirit to act, as at Pentecost, to shape timid followers into bold leaders.

...Elijah said to Elisha, "Tell me what I may do for you, before I am taken from you." Elisha said, "Please let me inherit a double share of your spirit."
2 KINGS 2:9

Pray for your successors in leadership. John 17 is a great example of the importance Jesus placed on praying for the next generation. Continue to pray for them.

The final step you must take in faith is to move on. Once the mentoring is over, and once the new generation of leaders is ready, the first generation must get out of the way. It will be very difficult and even painful; great faith will be required from all concerned.

As for me, ...the time for my departure has come. I have fought the good fight, I have finished the race, I have kept the faith.
2 TIMOTHY 4:6–7

It is human nature to doubt, so don't worry if all of this sounds unworkable in the complexity of the twenty-first century. It may help to remember that Jesus risked *everything* as He placed His very life on the line in passing the torch to His followers. After three years, He knew them intimately: especially their shortcomings, which were many. We can read about them twenty centuries later; Jesus saw them every day and knew their failings firsthand.

In the final moments of His earthly ministry, the risen Christ issued His only mandate to these awestruck followers: to do nothing less than change the world (Matthew 28: 18–20). His trust in the Father's plan must have been absolute to permit Him to depart under those circumstances. And you can be assured that His promise to be with them "to the end" passes on to you and your successors as well.

2
MONEY FOLLOWS PEOPLE

Lord, I too often try the easy path to fundraising. My attitude is that anyone who hears about our ministry should open up their purse and just pour out the money. Experience has taught me that it's not so automatic, and You continue to teach me that I need to invest in people, not in their checkbooks. Forgive me for treating people as nothing more than prospects. And help me to look deeper into the hearts and lives of others. Amen.

M oney fuels your ministry, just like a business enterprise. It is by no means the only resource, or even the most important one, but in one way or another it is essential.

Jesus may not have been a fundraiser in the way we think of today, but He did accept help, for example, from some women who "provided" for Him. Paul was a masterful fundraiser; if you read 2 Corinthians chapters 8 and 9 you'll notice him using tactics still employed today—like peer pressure.

Empty pockets never held anyone back.
Only empty heads and empty hearts can do that.
NORMAN VINCENT PEALE

You may attract donors or investors for a variety of reasons. Perhaps they give because of your friendship. Or possibly, they like your mission statement, your website, or your logo. Some respond out of guilt, while others might expect something in return from you.

But you are called to forge a deeper link with your supporters, one based on Christ Himself. Any seed that you scatter in the hope of a good return (good fruit) will fail unless it falls on the "good soil" which is Christ's soil. Only His soil will yield "thirty fold, sixty fold and a hundred fold."

Scripture teaches us that our treasure lines up with our hearts. As spiritual entrepreneurs, we are called to appeal to the heart and not just to the checkbook. That means that our behavior toward others must be based on more than their capacity to give. So our appeal to donors must reach into that deep place in their hearts where God Himself resides.

In two separate instances, Jesus instructed Peter to put his net out in a new spot: on the "right (other) side of the boat" or in the "deep water." And so must we. Conventional fundraising might mark this as folly. But you have an asset that the conventional fundraisers lack: the very Spirit of Christ, moving in the hearts of people who are reached by your mission and in your vision. And especially in the love that you demonstrate for your ministry and for the people you serve.

So even when we say along with Peter, "Master, we have worked all night long, and have caught nothing," we are not to doubt what Christ can do through us as "fishers of men." He brings the catch, but will not do so until we obey and put down the nets.

So put them down where He instructs: into the hearts of those He brings to you. You need not look elsewhere. And if those hearts reside in deep water do not be afraid. His catch will amaze you.

3
THE "NEXT LEVEL"

Lord, I hear about the "next level" as if it is some mythic place where all will be good. But honestly, I am struggling with *this* level, the place where we find ourselves today. Are we always supposed to aspire to bigger and better? There are so many voices, so many opinions screaming at me for something more, something different. How do I hear Your voice amidst the din? Please forgive me and help me with my frustration. Amen.

Perhaps Paul's letter to the early evangelists, outlining how to expand the young Christian community to the "next level" was lost in antiquity. In reality, most of his letters focused on holding on to the status quo, hoping to keep the new believers away from heresy and drift. His instructions on what we would call "evangelism" are non-existent.

This part of my life is all about embracing change and going to the next level, taking risks and showing my bravery.
BEYONCÉ

For most of us, the expression "the next level" describes a quantum leap, a giant step, or a new era. You will no doubt hear suggestions that the "next level" is a destination devoutly to be desired.

But in whose opinion? And what exactly is the next level anyway? Where does it belong in your spiritual adventure, where faith in the leading of the Father is the shaping force?

King David linked Israel and Judah and took the unified kingdom to the next level. Solomon held and expanded it; but corruption eroded the kingdom, and his heirs saw it disintegrate. The next level eventually fell.

Early missionary journeys of Paul and others took the fledgling Christian faith far from its home in Jerusalem to the ends of the known world. While not initially adding large numbers of followers, this next level served as the platform for the eventual growth of the church. It was a slow process with lots of ups and downs, and the next level wasn't reached in the lifetime of the first generation.

Our Lord is not against growth or the next level. On the contrary. He just wants to be in charge of it. We humans tend to force things, acting when we should be listening and following. We can tell ourselves that we are moving to the next level. When we do, we must ask how our efforts are honoring our Lord. Are we following Christ or are we trying to lead?

There is no evidence that Jesus considered the next level of any organization or church. Instead, He came to open up a personal "next level" to His children, the flock He came to shepherd and die for. For Him, moving to the next level was a story of resurrection and of bringing His children into His kingdom for all eternity.

What is the next level for the people you serve? It may be an educational attainment, better healthcare, safer streets, or food on the table. What is it for your board, volunteers, and donors? Whatever it is, you are called to strive for *their* next level and let our Lord take care of yours.

4
THE WEAK LINK

Lord, I do not have much patience with the weak links in this organization.
To me, they represent failure and I don't want any part of them. And I don't
want them to drag down others. So I either ignore them or worse, send
them subtle (or not so subtle) messages to dis-engage. They are not worth
my investment of time and energy. Please forgive my insensitivity and my
reluctance to see all Your children as precious in Your sight. Amen.

Organizations move at the pace of the slowest member, don't they?
Weak links are to be jettisoned as soon as they are identified, right?
Or so it might seem.

Who are the weak links in your ministry? They are easy to spot: those
who seem to wander away just when you need them, or who always seem
a bit lost, out of sync with you and others. You know them because they
have let you down and you've learned to avoid depending on them. And
you learned the hard way, through experience. Time after time they have
disappointed you.

Love is patient...
1 CORINTHIANS 13:4

Patience is the first attribute in Paul's definition of love. Consider that
for a moment. And consider your weak link in his or her fullest context:
not just what he or she can or cannot do for you and your ministry. Is
your weak link struggling with something? Dealing with a crisis of some
sort? A problem so deep that it hasn't been exposed?

All this is to say that, as a spiritual entrepreneur, you should be careful before throwing anyone away. Jesus never "fired" any of His weak links. Even Judas, who betrayed Him. Even Peter, who denied Him. Even Thomas, who doubted Him.

What do you think? If a shepherd has a hundred sheep, and one of them has gone astray, does he not leave the ninety-nine on the mountains and go in search of the one that went astray? And if he finds it, truly I tell you, he rejoices over it more than over the ninety-nine that never went astray.

MATTHEW 18:12–13

You may need to redirect a weak link to something more productive within his or her ability. You may need to redefine responsibilities, or provide some personal coaching. Finally, if all else fails, you may need to disconnect your weak link from your ministry.

But before you do, exhaust the avenues of love: listening, understanding, hoping, and forgiving. Remember: even you have been a weak link at times. Give your weak link direct but constructive counsel. Coach your weak link in the hope that improvement is possible.

Yours is a Christ-centered ministry. That doesn't mean that it's not accountable, or well run, or organized. It doesn't mean that your ministry doesn't deliver results, and it doesn't mean that you lead from weakness. Don't be afraid to have a difficult conversation.

But what does it mean to lead a Christ-centered ministry? Among other things, it means that your ministry reflects the fruits of the spirit: love, joy, peace, etc. It means that your ministry runs, as much as is humanly possible, in the image of Christ: full of love and mercy. And if the love must be tough love, then exercise that love with great tenderness.

5
CREATE A PIPELINE

Lord, I seem to always be in a hurry. Instant gratification is so
embedded in our culture, but I know that You did not live that way.
Can You weed it out of me? It leads my expectations out of the zone of reality
into a dream world where everything happens when and how I wish.
Please forgive me for wanting to get ahead of You and for trying to build
from the top down and not from the bottom up. Amen.

Early in your ministry, any source of funding and volunteers is pretty much fair game. So go ahead and pick the low-hanging fruit. It has been carefully placed in your path by the master planter. And you will truly be amazed at what our Lord will do to feed your ministry. Just harvest the fruit and give great thanks.

But you are in this for the long term, aren't you? And eventually, the low-hanging fruit will be picked clean. Many organizations plateau or even decline at this point, with leaders astonished at how hard it suddenly becomes. After taking full credit for the low-hanging fruit, they now look for someone or something to blame for the surprising challenges in resourcing the ministry.

The Israelites ate manna forty years, until they came to a habitable land;
they ate manna, until they came to the border of the land of Canaan.

EXODUS 16:35

Even as you enjoy the manna of first generation donors and volunteers, you must begin to cultivate the second generation. A pipeline is a great metaphor. It begins with an intake process then continues down a directed path toward increasing involvement, to a point where a new generation of donors and leaders emerges. As in a true pipeline, you should expect some leakage along the way.

Jesus' three-year ministry was almost wholly devoted to the pipeline. He gave literally all He had to the development of His surprisingly small band of uncredentialed followers. His pipeline has continued down the centuries to today, and is still active, producing generation after generation of Christian leaders.

I am the vine, you are the branches. Those who abide in me and I in them bear much fruit, because apart from me, you can do nothing.
JOHN 15:5

At the end of Jesus' three years with His disciples, and after suffering their betrayal and denial, Jesus might have despaired over the state of His pipeline. Most of us would have been terribly disappointed in them. We might have even required a final exam of sorts before departing. Those who failed would be weeded out.

But not Jesus. No final exam was needed to test His leaders. All Jesus asked of them can be summed up by His questions of Peter: "Do you love me? Do you love me? Do you love me?" He knew that the Holy Spirit would carry them through, into the next generation. As shaky as it looked, the pipeline was begun that would extend even into today and beyond. And so it will also be with you.

6
A SIGNATURE EVENT

Lord, no one knows about us. We have no image and no identity in the
community. What do we do? I feel lost, not knowing where to even begin.
And I am losing faith that this dream will ever succeed. I need some
encouragement. I need some direction. I need some patience.
I need a hug! Please forgive my lack of faith in You. Amen.

T he history of our faith has been marked by what we might today
call "signature events." What more dramatic event can you think
of than Passover? Even after three thousand years this event remains a
cornerstone of our faith.

*Jesus went throughout Galilee, teaching...and proclaiming...
and curing... So his fame spread...and they brought to him all the sick,
...and he cured them. And great crowds followed him...*
MATTHEW 4:23-25

Weren't these also signature events? And what about His feeding
thousands with just a few loaves and fishes? Even so, it is interesting to
note that while His "fame spread" through these signature events, and
they awed large crowds of witnesses, they did not produce loyal followers, i.e. disciples. The events may have put Jesus on the map with thousands, but most of the witnesses quickly resumed their lives, impressed
but unmoved. In fact, it was only the *opponents* of Jesus who acted on
what they saw and heard, determining that He had to be stopped.

But not all of His signature events were witnessed by crowds. Some were more intimate; ironically, they are remembered perhaps even more than His widely-witnessed miracles. The meal that Jesus shared in an upper room with His twelve closest followers has become one of our most treasured sacraments. His transfiguration, witnessed by only three, is seen as remarkable evidence of His divinity. And, of course, only a handful of women were the first to see our Risen Lord. These smaller events, together with another at Pentecost, seemed to be much more effective in developing disciples.

What does all of this mean in the context of your ministry? Do you need to establish yourself with an attention-grabbing event that will attract crowds? Yes, you probably do, especially if you are serving a hard-to-penetrate community. And while you are thinking about it, consider partnering with another organization better known than you, and ride their coattails until you are more established in the community.

You are the light of the world.
MATTHEW 5:14

But don't forget the more intimate signature events. A small prayer service can be especially meaningful. Likewise, visits to the hospital, mentoring a student, or cleaning up an empty lot. These may not make the headlines, but they tend to cement your culture of love and service in the hearts of those present.

And in the long run, these more intimate signature events and activities will shape your organization from the inside out. They may just help you build a team of loyal followers. Why? Because they occur at a personal level, allowing God's love to flow from one human heart to another. In these personal signature events those who serve, together with those who are served, will see the face of Christ.

Yet such is oft the course of deeds that move the wheels of the world: small hands do them because they must, while the eyes of the great are elsewhere.

J.R.R. TOLKIEN, THE LORD OF THE RINGS

7
LEARNING AS YOU GO

Lord, I lead from what I perceive to be my strengths. But I can't limit myself to the few areas where I am strong. As You know, my range of strengths is pretty narrow. I need to perform well in so many areas of leadership, not just those where I am comfortable. Somewhere in all of this, it seems that I should be acting more out of faith and moving out of my comfort zone. Can You give me the faith to do that? Amen.

The personality tests that you have taken provide abundant data on your strengths and weaknesses. Their underlying message is clear: lead from your strengths and if possible, avoid anything that would draw on or expose your weaknesses.

Are you a good planner and deep thinker? That's good. But what happens when all you do is plan and think? Actually nothing happens, because there is no action. Sooner or later you must stop planning and thinking and begin to act. You can't just sit back, plan and think, then disappear when it's time to act. For a young organization, it's *always* time to act.

What if you are, in fact, a more action-oriented leader? If that is all you feel comfortable doing, you can spin yourself into a frenzy of action with no plan, no direction and no thought of the consequences. Trusting others to do the planning and thinking for you will lead to trouble. Who will you blame when your poorly planned actions go awry?

The obvious answer is balance. Planners and thinkers must learn to lead in action, learning as they go. Action-oriented types must learn to stop every so often and consider their past actions and next steps. The balance then becomes a learning loop. For a planner/thinker, the experience gained from action feeds into better plans and deeper thought. And when an action-oriented leader slows down long enough to think about his or her actions, they become more focused and productive.

Trust God that you are exactly where you are meant to be.
TERESA OF ÁVILA

You cannot stop learning. But learning is more than attending seminars and reading articles. Those are fine, but you must be an on-the-ground leader, one who leads not so much from strength, but instead, from faith. Let our Lord decide how to use *all* of your strengths, including those lesser strengths that you consider weaknesses.

My grace is sufficient for you, for my power is made perfect in weakness.
2 CORINTHIANS 12: 9

We don't know what Paul's thorn in the flesh was. Whatever it was, his prayer to have it removed was answered in the passage above. It was not answered in the way he would have preferred. But in great faith, Paul answered the Risen Christ:

So, I will boast all the more gladly of my weaknesses,
so that the power of Christ may dwell in me.
2 CORINTHIANS 12:9

We can fret and moan about our perceived weaknesses. But the power of Christ is stronger than our weaknesses. Let Him use you, *all of you,* in great faith.

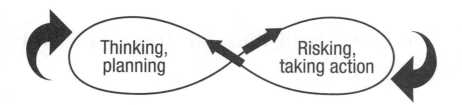

The infinity loop above graphically represents how we (ideally) learn and grow. Thinking should lead, not to even more thinking, but to action, which then produces the experience on which our thinking and judgment improve. Likewise, risking and taking action should lead, not to even more action, but to pausing to stop and consider the results. As a consequence, we can improve the future effectiveness of both our thinking and our action as they feed one another. To do otherwise leads to polarization on one side or other of the loop.

This concept of the infinity closed loop is thoroughly and insightfully explored by Opposite Strengths (http://www.oppositestrengths.com/), an executive coaching service that has been transformational for me.

8
TEST EVERYTHING; HOLD ON TO WHAT IS GOOD

Lord, I must not have a very discerning mind. I chase too many things and when I hit a dead end, find myself stymied by the challenge of backing up and starting over. Forgive me for not looking to You and for not trusting Your lead, as well as the counsel of those who You've called to lead with me. At the end of the day, I seem to lack a clear definition of what You would call good. Please forgive me and guide me. Amen.

W e follow a God of abundance. Opportunities appear like flowers bursting forth in springtime. Your fertile mind produces a new idea about every fifteen seconds. And of course, you have been called to use your gift of saying "yes," so you want to chase each and every one! But some of your ideas are not all that good, and you can't say "yes" to everything. If you do, you will quickly learn that pursuing all paths at once can get you into serious trouble.

. . . It is presumptuous in me to wish to choose my path,
because I cannot tell which path is best for me. I must leave it to the Lord,
who knows me, to lead me by the path which is best for me,
so that in all things his will may be done.
TERESA OF ÁVILA

We do have to make choices. Don't be ashamed or embarrassed to conclude that a new idea is too big for a young organization to undertake. Don't overextend so much that your companions become discouraged from the weight of your vision. Don't be afraid to stockpile some of your best ideas for the future, while you pursue the paths of the present.

So what is "good?" There is no magic formula for discerning what is good. But the advice to "test everything" can serve you well. So how do you do it? Here are some ideas:

- Pray for God's wisdom in the paths you choose to follow. *In particular, prayer in community can be a powerful force in discernment.* Include your inner circle, partners, and even some in the community at large. You may be too close to or too proud of your own ideas to discern alone.
- Practice patience. Sensitize yourself to wait for the gentle whisper of the Spirit. Wait for the counsel of those who our Lord has provided to you, for just this purpose. Avoid the impulse of your own ego.
- Pursue His advice to test everything. That means monitoring your progress as you go, right from the beginning. A door that appeared wide open at first may lead to a dead end. Or it may lead to something totally new and unexpected, 180 degrees from what you originally envisioned. Don't be afraid to change course, to allow your idea to morph into what the Father had in mind from the beginning.

We like to say that only God can define success. If so, then the inverse must also be true: only God can define failure. What you may consider failure (or what other voices tell you is failure) may be exactly what God has in mind. Don't be too quick to judge, at least not until you prayerfully consider what may be the "unintended consequences" of your "bad idea."

Place what you consider a failure into God's hands. See what He will do with it. Your failure may be a necessary stepping stone to God's master plan for good.

VII.
SPIRITUAL SUCCESS

Without a doubt, the biggest challenge I have faced with Newspring is maintaining its spiritual focus. Faith-based organizations tend to drift. It happens. And when you look at many faith-based organizations, it's hard to detect any spiritual vitality at all. A prayer to open a meeting may be the only evidence in many cases.

When the spiritual emphasis fades, the energy of the entire mission fades with it. Before long, the ministry is not what it was founded to be. And when that happens, the people involved in the ministry can display vastly different motivations.

Keep perspective on the spiritual foundation of your ministry, and focus on how to preserve and grow it. You should expect a story of ups and downs. At Newspring, we have experienced both deaths and resurrections along the way. And I can say that I have personally experienced some of my own deaths and resurrections. But that is the journey that our Lord calls us to. All we can do is pick up our cross and walk with Him.

When it's so difficult to maintain a spiritual focus, why even try? There are so many other challenges to face.

Why? Because of the incomparable joy of walking with Christ. And not only with Him, but also with the others who He calls to walk with you. The biggest blessing of Newspring to me has been the gift of brothers and sisters in Christ who walk with me. These are people who He has called to His journey (never my journey), to walk the road of ministry, to share the ups and downs, the deaths and resurrections along the way. This gift is the most precious thing you can gain from your calling to ministry. I would not trade it for anything.

1
THE COMMON DENOMINATOR

Lord, I get caught up in so many things, so many details,
it sometimes overwhelms me. So much to accomplish. Trails of
opportunity lead off in all directions. But every now and then I am reminded
that Your purpose underlies everything I am called to do. You truly are the
common denominator, the foundation of it all. You bring it all
together in a way I mostly fail to understand. Please forgive me for
complicating Your calling in so many ways. Amen.

Your strategic plan (if you have one) looks out into the future, defining the paths and projects you intend to follow. God has a plan too, and your spiritual adventure is part of it. Each individual who is a part of your adventure, as well as anyone impacted by it, into future generations, is also part of God's plan.

We humans tend to think in a linear fashion, cause and effect: step A leads to step B, which produces a desired outcome. When the outcome doesn't turn out as expected, we trace back the steps to see what went wrong.

Then they said, "Come, let us build ourselves a city, and a tower with its top in the heavens, and let us make a name for ourselves... "
GENESIS 11:4

But our Lord isn't bound by linear thinking; and, in Him, everything belongs. He uses all of it. We may not see where some things fit, including the unintended consequences that appear as if from nowhere. Can we see where our own missteps fit His plan? Not likely. God not only sees, He actually uses it all to achieve His will. Nothing is lost, nothing wasted.

God's will is that no bounds should be set to his works.
TERESA OF ÁVILA

So what is the common denominator? What is the thread that runs through everything? It is nothing less than the love of God as expressed in Christ's life, death and resurrection. His is the highest possible calling, and He connects everything, even though we don't always see how.

And how does God's common denominator translate into your spiritual adventure? It happens one person at a time, as lives are changed. Your spiritual adventure is nothing less than a vessel carrying pilgrims like yourself forward into personal stories of God's incredible love.

So if you are trying to build a monument that reaches to the heavens, know that God is already reaching down to you and your companions on your spiritual adventure. You, and all of you, are making up the raw materials for His work, which truly knows no bounds.

He will be in your strategic plan. You cannot keep Him out of it. He will be in your day-to-day activities, whether you know it or not. He will be in your victories and also in your defeats. He will be in every email, every word spoken, every volunteer hour, every board meeting. It will be up to you to recognize Him, to witness to Him and to love Him.

Our Lord is the common denominator of everything.

2
WHO IS THIS *REALLY* FOR?

Lord, I keep getting surprised by the direction this adventure is taking.
Control, at least control by me, is becoming something of a joke.
Things keep happening that I didn't plan. Stories of transformation
continue to bubble up in the most unusual places. What is it all about, really?
Is there some great truth that is higher than our mission statement?
Please forgive my myopic view of this spiritual adventure
and help me to see as You see. Amen.

Maybe this is a weird question: who is this *really* for?
The obvious answer is that it's for the people you serve, the ones who have some kind of need, perhaps the people who Jesus termed "the least of these." And of course, there is no shortage of people in need. Part of your original motivation might have been a holy discontent about the plight of a certain population. There are plenty to go around.

Secular service organizations abound with aid to the needy. They play an essential role in delivering services of all kinds in all places. But your calling goes deeper, to the heart of your spiritual adventure. And not only yours, but also that of your board, volunteers, donors, and of the people you serve.

Jesus was not a man for others. He was one with others.
There is a world of difference in that. He didn't champion the cause
of the outcast. He was the outcast.
GREGORY BOYLE, TATTOOS ON THE HEART

So the question "Who is this really for?" is not so simple. The spiritual dimension of your adventure will penetrate into its very life, from day-to-day activities to board meetings, retreats, budget activities, and more. In short, the spiritual dimension is all-encompassing. You are not to merely deliver services; you are to be one with those you serve, just as Christ is one with the outcast and the marginalized.

That's why you experience so many unintended consequences. It's why you discover so many stories of transformation outside of your stated mission, and outside of the population you serve. It's why you feel such a bond with those who share this adventure with you.

You see, Jesus didn't just instruct His followers to simply serve the "least of these." He could have stopped there. But He didn't. Jesus went on to say that when you do serve the "least of these" then *you are serving Christ Himself.* That makes a huge difference! He has made it personal. It means that His life is fully embedded in your service, connecting you to Him as you serve. It gives your service a spiritual, perhaps even sacred dimension that goes deeper than the act of service itself.

---

*And the king will answer them, "Truly I tell you, just as you did it to one of the least of these who are members of my family, **you did it to me.**"*
MATTHEW 25:40

It all connects: your service, those whom you serve, your companions, and your spiritual journey. They are inseparable from our Lord. *He calls you to claim the connection!*

3
YOUR ADVENTURE IS PART OF A RESURRECTION STORY

Lord, I really don't know what tomorrow might bring. This entire adventure has been so unpredictable that I have given up attempting to see too far down the road, much less manage it. Perhaps that's what You've wanted all along. Is the unpredictability part of the adventure? Even so, part of me still wants to control it, and I am still driven to succeed and to look good in the process. Please forgive me for dwelling on my own story and neglecting You and the stories of others. Amen.

W hose resurrection story? Theirs or yours?

A resurrection story suggests a death and a rebirth, a new life in Christ. And where can you find stories of new life? You can find them in the lives of those you serve.

Resurrection stories will abound in your ministry: stories of people who have been called back from the depths of depression, who've been given a second chance, whose lives have been turned around by acts of love, compassion, and mercy. Broken relationships are healed, people are fed and educated, and energy for life is restored, all by the mysterious movement of the Spirit. And all transmitted through Christ's love expressed by you and your companions on your spiritual adventure.

So listen to their stories: the stories of death and resurrection. They may not be so obvious on the surface. Once you get to know your ministry at a personal level, though, they will crystallize into a picture of God at work. Those you serve will truly appear with the face of Christ. And you will witness the Spirit of Christ at work in the world.

But what about you and your companions on the journey? Does your spiritual adventure have room for a personal resurrection story? Yes it does.

When you see other lives changed, does your own life change? When you see and experience the love of Christ through your work, are you given hope? Faith? Does your prayer time come alive with the energy of the Spirit? Do brothers and sisters in Christ rise up to share your spiritual adventure? Yes, that is what you can expect.

But there is more. What about your "death?" What dies before your resurrection? For you, the death will take some form of a loss of control. It may involve the death of that false self of yours that must always succeed, always win and always look good in leadership.

What dies will be replaced by a recognition that it is only in Christ that you will find any success, and that your desire is for Him to "look good" even when you do not.

It's a recognition, deep inside of you, that life in Christ is more precious than looking good. Nothing else will do as you finally discard that false self in exchange for life in Him, which is nothing less than the true self that He created for you long ago.

> *The path of dying and rising is exactly what any in-depth spiritual teaching must aim for.*
> **RICHARD ROHR**

And what about your "resurrection?"

It's much more than witnessing the changed lives of others. Once you die to control and to your false self, you need no longer fear that your life might never attain a true relevance, a real significance and meaning. When you once feared that someday your life would dead-end in emptiness, you can you now be assured that Christ's call to this spiritual adventure has truly raised you to new life.

4
FOR HIS NAME'S SAKE

Lord, I am lackadaisical about Your name and about giving You the glory for this spiritual adventure. Mostly I just forget. Don't take it personally. But sometimes I figuratively elbow You out of the way so that I can take center stage. Please forgive both my intentional and unintentional slights to you. You are the life, heart and Lord of everything. Amen.

Do you know how many references there are in scripture to "His name" or "your name" or "my name"? Probably more than you might imagine. Here are a few:

But to all who received him, who believed in his name,
he gave power to become children of God, ...
JOHN 1:12

When he was in Jerusalem during the Passover festival, many believed
in his name because they saw the signs that he was doing.
JOHN 2:23

Father, glorify your name. Then a voice came from heaven,
"I have glorified it, and I will glorify it again."
JOHN 12:28

But the Advocate, the Holy Spirit, whom the Father will send in my name,
will teach you everything, and remind you of all that I have said to you.
JOHN 14:26

*You did not choose me but I chose you. And I appointed you
to go and bear fruit, fruit that will last, so that the
Father will give you whatever you ask him in my name.*

JOHN 15:16

*But these are written so that you may come to believe that Jesus is the Messiah,
the Son of God, and that through believing you may have life in his name.*

JOHN 20:31

These are just a few from the Gospel of John. Elsewhere in the Gospels we hear about welcoming a child, being hated, receiving prophets, casting out demons, giving the Gentiles hope, gathering one or two together, leaving families and homes, baptizing, offering a cup of water, *all in His name.*

So how does this apply to your spiritual adventure? As a Christ-centered ministry, you are to honor our Lord's name. But how? Are you to take your spiritual fervor to the streets in His name? Should you be evangelistic, piling up conversions in His name? Should you advertise His name on billboards?

Only you can answer these questions. Whatever you do should be "contextual" which is to say that it should be reflective of the community you serve, its spiritual makeup and values.

Pray about it. Consult others. But be intentional. Don't be ashamed of our Lord, the giver of life to both you and your spiritual adventure. "Test everything" and don't be afraid to try something new. Let everyone connected to you know where you stand.

---

*There is always the danger that we may just do the work
for the sake of the work. This is where the respect and the love and the
devotion come in—that we do it to God, to Christ, and that's
why we try to do it as beautifully as possible.*

MOTHER TERESA

5
THE LEAVES VS THE FRUIT

Lord, I understand that You are all about fruit. You are the vine, we are the branches and we are to produce fruit. But sometimes, I just produce leaves and hope that they will pass for fruit. I know that upon closer inspection, it will be apparent that the fruit is missing. I know too, that You are able to produce fruit in and through me even out of season. Please forgive my lack of faith and my pretending that I produce fruit when really it's only leaves. Amen.

The plain fact is that (only) in Christ, can we produce fruit, in *or* out of season. He frees us from the perceived limitations that have always held us back. These are our "mental models," many of which were formed in childhood. *"I could never do that. It's not my strength. That's too difficult. Too risky. Too undefined. Out of my comfort zone."*

These mental models seek to pilot our path through life. They appear as convention, tradition, and rational thought. They feed our false selves.

Christ breaks their hold on us, if we will believe in Him. And so in Christ we *can* produce fruit where and when we thought impossible.

In the morning as they passed by, they saw the fig tree withered away to its roots. Then Peter remembered and said to him, "Rabbi, look! The fig tree that you cursed has withered." Jesus answered them, "Have faith in God. Truly I tell you, if you say to this mountain, 'Be taken up and thrown into the sea,' and if you do not doubt in your heart, but believe that what you say will come to pass, it will be done for you. So I tell you, whatever you ask for in prayer, believe that you have received it, and it will be yours.

MARK 11:20–24

Consider the twelve. Time after time their prevailing response was "no" while Jesus said "yes." Time after time He stretched their minds and hearts to believe that in Him, all things truly are possible. Time after time He *showed* them what was possible in Him, if they would only believe.

So who really is the fig tree? Whose branches bear attractive leaves but no fruit? Who is unprepared for the King when He approaches? Who is attempting to live out a spiritual adventure from inside a self-defined comfort zone? Who is finding it hard to believe that in Christ, all things truly are possible? If it's you, remember His perseverance with the twelve. He never gave up on them. Even to the point of His own death. Neither will He give up on you! Let Him encourage and strengthen you.

I can do all things through him who strengthens me.
PHILIPPIANS 4:13

Your role as a spiritual entrepreneur is not just to live this out for yourself in your own imperfect way. You are also called to encourage others in your ministry who suffer from the bonds of their own personal mental models. Be a part of the Spirit's work to free them to believe that they can bear fruit in all seasons!

6
YOUR PART VS GOD'S PART

Lord, where do You end and I begin? I fear that sometimes I am overstepping and at other times I am holding back. Everything feels so awkward, so un-coordinated in trying to follow You. Your Word is pretty clear but also kind of abstract. I need practical help in specific circumstances. When it doesn't come, my tendency is to act. But I am so clumsy! Waiting on You has always been hard. Please forgive me. Amen.

It is a myth to think that God works alongside of us. In fact, He works *within* us, and also within others.

Now to him who by the power at work within us is able to accomplish abundantly far more than all we can ask or imagine, to him be the glory in the church and in Christ Jesus to all generations, forever and ever.
EPHESIANS 3:20-21.

So when God works within us, who is actually doing the work? It's a mystery of the Spirit and further, it's pretty pointless to try to sort it out and rationalize it. Jesus used the metaphor of fruit, and He calls us to bear much of it. Only in Christ are we able to bear fruit. And He emphasizes that we are the ones to bear the fruit, and His role is to feed us (He is the vine and we are the branches).

But what exactly is flowing from the vine to the branches and into our fruit? Is it know-how? Strategy? Energy? Technique?

It's love. Love powers and motivates everything. It is the currency of His kingdom, the vocabulary of His language. He is the author and source of it, a deep well that provides an eternal and unlimited supply.

Well, finally... it isn't a matter of reason. Finally, it's a matter of love.
SIR THOMAS MORE IN A MAN FOR ALL SEASONS

So God doesn't really end where you begin. He doesn't end at all. He is in you and also in others and in all of creation. He is a life force, actually *the* life force. You will find God in everything you do. He's not just a part of your "to-do" list. He is in each and every item on it. We can't separate Him from us in the work He has called us to.

Many people mistake our work for our vocation.
Our vocation is the love of Jesus.
MOTHER TERESA

So when you look back, it's tempting to ask, "What did God do and what did I do?" As some will say, you can see God's handprints every-where. But even where you cannot see them, He was there. Even in the dark places, He was there. In the times of confusion, the perceived set-backs and failures, He was there, working toward love, and working at a depth of mystery that you may not see, at least not immediately. Consider the words of Joseph:

Even though you intended to do harm to me, God intended it for good,
in order to preserve a numerous people, as he is doing today.
GENESIS 50:20

7
PURE? NOTHING IS PURE EXCEPT GOD

Lord, this is something I need to get over: my feeling of impurity and the damage it does. Maybe I'm listening to the wrong voice. It's a voice that tells me that I am unfit because my motives aren't totally pure, and my faith isn't what it should be. And it's true. I do this for You, but I also do it for me. Please forgive my lack of faith and my mixed motives. Amen.

I f we are not careful, this feeling of impurity can literally paralyze us. The need to measure up to some abstract standard, and the recognition of our personal impurity and lack of faith can subvert our very calling. We truly live in "clay jars."

Immediately the father of the child cried out, "I believe; help my unbelief!"
MARK 9:24

Scripture is full of individuals we would consider giants of the faith. Begin with Abraham (who prostituted his own wife), then Jacob (a deceiver and thief), Moses (a murderer) and David (an adulterer and murderer). And of course, Rahab the prostitute. New Testament giants fare no better: Peter (who denied Jesus) and Paul (persecutor of the faith). Mary Magdalene apparently had a reputation. Read 2 Corinthians 11 to get a picture of Paul's mixed motives. His personal jealousy comes through loud and clear.

The important work of moving the world forward
does not wait to be done by perfect men.
GEORGE ELLIOT

Nevertheless, each one was called to significant ministry. Each one was imperfect, impure. And yet each one responded to the call in faith. Could they say "no?"

Christ calls us where we are, in the midst of our impurity. There are no pre-conditions; there is no job interview, no application to fill out and no admission test. Jesus never said that we are to love our neighbor once we had met some prerequisites. He never called us to serve the least of these only after completing rites of purification. And He never instructed us to make disciples based on our having first earned a PhD in holiness.

Holiness does not consist in doing extraordinary things.
It consists in accepting, with a smile, what Jesus sends us.
It consists in accepting and following the will of God
MOTHER TERESA

Let's state it clearly: One great idea of the biblical revelation is that God is manifest in the ordinary, in the actual, in the daily, in the now, in the concrete incarnations of life, and not through purity codes and moral achievement contests, which are seldom achieved anyway.
RICHARD ROHR

Purity of motive is not about you. Nothing is pure but God alone.

8
GOD ALWAYS BEGINS AT THE BOTTOM

Lord, I catch myself drifting into dreams of greatness (for me).
I want to associate with the rich and powerful, and I tell myself that it's okay
because it's all for good. My daydreams elevate me to rock-star status.
When I wake up I realize how far I have drifted from You.
When I see myself with the rich and powerful, I see You standing
with the poor and afflicted. Please forgive me. Amen.

I s it human nature for us to aspire to the top? To wish for greatness?
To pursue power? After all, with power, we could do so much good for
the world.

*Jesus...got up from the table, took off his outer robe, and tied a towel
around himself. Then he poured water into a basin and began to wash the
disciples' feet and to wipe them with the towel that was tied around him.*
JOHN 13:3-5

Upward mobility is a hallmark of American culture. Stories of ambition and success abound in our literature, from biographies to business
magazines to websites.

What's wrong with ambition and success? What's wrong with upward mobility?

The story of our salvation stands radically over and against
the philosophy of upward mobility. The great paradox which Scripture
reveals to us is that real and total freedom is only found through downward
mobility. The Word of God came down to us and lived among us
as a slave. The divine way is indeed the downward way.

HENRI NOUWEN

We cannot deny our human nature. Even if humility is foreign to us, a model of it has been provided in the life of Christ. And not only in His life, but in the lives of those He associated with and called to follow Him: uneducated fishermen, a tax collector, women of questionable repute, all middle class or lower.

Jesus could have called the rich and powerful. Did He call members of the Sanhedrin? Were any of the Roman elite among His followers? Anyone from the Jewish aristocracy?

Do you wish to rise? Begin by descending. You plan a tower
that will pierce the clouds? Lay first the foundation of humility.

ST. AUGUSTINE

But don't we need donors? Partners? Leaders? Yes of course we do, and we can no more exclude the rich and powerful than the poor and weak.

It all comes down to humility, a quality that needs to be practiced in order to be mastered. Associating only with the rich and powerful makes humility practically impossible. Practicing downward mobility with one and all allows us to stand with Christ. You will always find Him with the poor and weak. Ask Him to guide you.

And all of you must clothe yourselves with humility
in your dealings with one another.

1 PETER 5:5

9
WAITING ON GOD

Lord, I have to say that this spiritual adventure has taught me (some) patience. But I still have so far to go! Waiting on You is the hardest part of all. And I must admit that so often I get frustrated waiting on You, only to discover that You were active all along, working where I wasn't looking. Please forgive my impatience and also my blindness. Amen.

Can you actually see God working? It's hard. Knowing where to look seems to be the key. Otherwise, we can seemingly wait forever, losing patience rather than growing it.

Stories about waiting on God abound in scripture. Abraham and Sarah waited decades for the birth of Isaac. Jacob labored fourteen years to finally marry Rachel. Joseph endured years in an Egyptian prison. The children of Israel wandered forty years in the wilderness.

Even youths shall faint and be weary, and young men shall
fall exhausted; but they who wait for the LORD shall renew their strength;
they shall mount up with wings like eagles;
they shall run and not be weary; they shall walk and not faint.
ISAIAH 40:30-33

But is waiting on God really nothing more than sitting around passively, hoping for something good to happen? Is it endlessly praying for a heavenly infusion of patience and obedience? Surely, it's much, much more.

But Jesus answered them, "My Father is still working,
and I also am working."
JOHN 5:17

In truth, God is never inactive. He is always working, but not necessarily in plain view, and not necessarily where we expect to see Him.

Waiting on God requires a vision of sorts. When we wait on Him we must suspend our human vision and begin to see spiritually. So look for God working in the hearts of the lonely, the dispossessed, and the weak. Look for Him working, not only at the center of your ministry, but also on its fringes. Look for Him as He softens hearts you thought could never be reached. Suspend your rules of cause and effect and look to see His blessings where the only possible cause is His loving grace.

Waiting on God is attitudinal. It's not an excuse for passivity. But it means that we must intentionally stop and look, considering the possibility that God's agenda is different and far greater than ours. It means that we must put aside our priorities and embrace His.

Biblically, waiting is not just something we have to do until we get what we want. Waiting is part of the process of becoming what God wants us to be.
JOHN ORTBERG

And yes, waiting on God does teach patience. It means hanging on when we just don't get it, when we simply can't see Him, or when the best we can do is to see from a distance, or through a glass, darkly.

The first chapter of book of Acts chronicles the final meeting between the Risen Christ and His followers. Of all the questions they might have asked, this is what they did ask: *"Lord, is this the time when you will restore the kingdom to Israel?"*

Clearly, after three years, they still didn't get it. But we must give them credit for this: they hung on, waiting on God. And when Jesus' promise of the coming of the Advocate was fulfilled and the Holy Spirit came upon them at Pentecost, they finally saw what He had been doing all along.

So it will be with you in your spiritual adventure. You may be slow to see God working, but hang on. His faith in you is greater than yours in Him. He will not desert you. Ever.

VIII.
ENCOURAGEMENT

have a strong need for encouragement. In many ways I am a self-starter, but that doesn't mean that I can go for long without (positive) feedback. And when my encouragement tank runs low, I can become a different person, striving to win the praise of pretty much anyone and everyone. It's hard to admit, but it's true. And while I am at it, I might as well also admit that my encouragement tank doesn't hold very much; it runs dry pretty quickly. You might even say that I am addicted to encouragement. And that addiction can easily turn into jealousy, greed, and any number of other qualities that I wish I didn't have.

Our Lord knows all of this, and I am grateful that He doesn't shut me out as a result. On the contrary, He has generously raised up people who express His encouragement for me, often in surprising ways. And in the process, He also has taught me a few things.

First, our Lord has taught me to not question the sources or the means of encouragement. If it fails to come from those I seek, or in the form or expression I prefer, I still must value it. Many times I have been surprised at the source of encouragement, just as I have been disappointed that those from whom I seek encouragement have not provided it. But I'm reminded almost daily that God is in charge of the Encouragement Department and He will dispense it as He pleases. If I try too hard to make it happen, my effort tarnishes the experience of hearing it.

Second, He has taught me to be available for encouragement that follows His ways instead of my expectations. That means that I must listen for His word. So like St. Francis, I look to unlikely places like nature, the poor and weak, the stranger, bystander, etc. to hear our Lord express His words of encouragement. And, finally, I am learning to find encouragement inside, from that voice that whispered to me in the first place, and which still whispers if I will but hear Him.

I hope that you find comfort about the faithfulness of our Lord in encouraging you. He will give you what you need. And He will teach you so much if you will humble yourself and listen for His word.

1
WHY DOES THE HIGH ROAD FEEL SO LOW?

Lord, I truly am trying to follow You, but I feel lost and in the dark much of the time. Where's the light? And it's true, loving all of my companions should be a big part of this spiritual adventure. But, sometimes, personalities clash and opinions conflict. And even when I act in a way that I think would please You, I feel drained and low. Then, I don't feel like trying the high road any longer. I just want to win. Or hide. Please forgive me. Amen.

What is your vision of the high road? For many, the high road is a place of clarity, where we can see where we're going. And it's also a place of grace, where patience and peace reign, even in the face of disagreements and animosity. The high road was so easy at the beginning of our spiritual adventure. But as the adventure has unfolded, it has become more difficult. Why is it so hard?

First, consider the challenges you face. Your calling arrived on a cloudy day and it hasn't gotten much clearer since. The community you serve is mired in many problems, some quite deep and stubborn. What is the best way to help? It's hard to see.

And what about your companions on this spiritual adventure? They were so great at first. But over time, friction develops, and it gets harder to stay on the high road. Going from good to bad to worse, you may be misunderstood, vilified, undermined, unappreciated, marginalized, and more. It is inescapable, unless you can find an environment totally free of humanity's potential for darkness. The high road has gotten slippery and unsafe.

There are no safe paths in this part of the world. Remember you are over the Edge of the Wild now, and in for all sorts of fun wherever you go.

J.R.R. TOLKIEN

Is it true? Have you left any safe path far behind? Is there no way to keep to the high road and not get hurt in the process? Are you destined to slog it out in the darkness?

If a man wishes to be sure of the road he treads on, he must close his eyes and walk in the dark.

ST. JOHN OF THE CROSS

Then close your eyes and let God lead you. Even, and most especially, in the dark. Even, and most especially, when it feels like you have slipped off the high road.

When clouds cover the light and you are in the dark, God is at work in you. He isn't necessarily smoothing your path, and He isn't waving a magic wand of grace over your companions. *He's working on you.* On the inside. Doing what, you may ask?

He is loosening your grip on attachments. Are you too entrenched in defending your personal vision? He will work to loosen your attachment and build your faith in Him. Is looking good overly important to you? He will work to turn you to humility. Have results and metrics become your god? He will soften your heart and turn you toward love. Are you fixated on being right all the time? He will loosen your grip and sensitize you to the opinions of others. You won't see Him working. Just stay in the cover of the darkness that our Lord provides and close your eyes. God does His best work when you are on the low road.

2
MANY TURNED AWAY, BUT PETER SAID,
"YOU HAVE THE WORDS OF ETERNAL LIFE"

Lord, I am discovering that this spiritual adventure is not for everyone.
Some are turning away because it's too uncertain, too undefined,
or not what they expected. I worry it's because we try so hard
to maintain a faith-based approach. Thanks to You, at least some of us are
experiencing a deeper life in You, Lord, as a result;
we wouldn't trade it for anything! I just wish I could say that for everyone.
Have I done something wrong? If so, please forgive me. Amen.

Jesus has just finished speaking of the need for His followers to eat His flesh and drink His blood. If they don't, He says, they will have no life in Him. For many, it's a very hard saying.

Because of this many of his disciples turned back and no longer
went about with him. So Jesus asked the twelve, "Do you also wish to go
away?" Simon Peter answered him, "Lord, to whom can we go?
You have the words of eternal life. We have come to believe and
know that you are the Holy One of God."
JOHN 6:66–69

Choosing to live in faith and follow Christ can be every bit as polarizing in the twenty-first century as it was in the first century.

Jesus clearly wasn't selling anything. Nothing was sugar-coated to make it sound better. And yet Peter would not be shaken, nor would at least ten other followers. They may not have understood exactly what Jesus meant, but they knew one big thing: He offered life, and there was something about Him that made them believe.

Peter didn't just claim that Jesus offered a better deal than other prophets, nor did he claim that Jesus was smarter, more charismatic, or more attractive in any way. And he certainly didn't claim that any financial or social advantages might come to him because he followed Jesus. On the contrary, Peter often heard Jesus warn of the dangers in following him.

No, Peter felt something in Jesus that connected with his soul in a more profound way than words could ever describe. He could only say that despite all the uncertainty and warnings of danger, he believed that Jesus was the Holy One of God.

And so it is with you. If following Christ in great faith alienates some, let it be so. Perhaps their time will come later. Don't give up on the life that *you* find in Christ. It is precious. Open the door to that life as you feel led in your spiritual adventure. Share it with as many as will drink from the eternal springs of Christ.

This is what you are to do: lift your heart up to the Lord, with a gentle stirring of love desiring him for his own sake and not for his gifts. Center all your attention and desire on him and let this be the sole concern of your mind and heart. Do all in your power to forget everything else, keeping your thoughts and desires free from any involvement with any of God's creatures or their affairs whether in general or particular. Perhaps this will seem like an irresponsible attitude, but I tell you, let them all be; pay no attention to them.
THE CLOUD OF UNKNOWING

3
WHEN YOU ARE NOT IN CONTROL

Lord, I was taught to be in control. All of the time. And if I wasn't
in control, I was supposed to look as if I was. But this spiritual adventure is
teaching me otherwise. It's painful and I am afraid that I don't react too well
when it's obvious that I've lost control. Please forgive my lack
of faith and my unwillingness to let go. Amen.

It won't take long for you to realize that you are seldom in control of anything. At least not like you'd like to be. Sometimes, when you are more present to the leading of God, it can actually exhilarate you, feeling like you are surfing on a wave not of your own creation. All too often, though, it feels like drowning in a sea of disappointment and downright fear.

Dionysius, a sixth century mystical theologian, said that we start the spiritual path thinking that we are pulling on a chain that is attached to heaven. Only midway in the journey do we realize that the chain that we thought we were pulling is instead pulling us—to an alluring brilliance.

RICHARD ROHR

You live in the paradox of existence as a leader *and* follower, someone in charge but also a servant. Others expect you to display strength, authority and control. But God is looking for obedience and humility. It is a tension that twists you in opposing directions.

I do not want to foresee the future. I am concerned with taking care of the present. God has given me no control over the moment following.

MAHATMA GANDHI

So do you suffer from a lack of control? No doubt you do and "suffer" is the best word to describe how it feels. We think of suffering followers of Christ: martyrs and victims of persecution, like you find in Hebrews chapter 11. Is your suffering in their league?

Probably not. And yet your loss of control is suffering indeed. It feels like failure and defeat. And it goes against all the conditioning you have received from your education, career and any leadership training you've ever attended. Even your coach will tell you that control is good.

Read Paul's letters to get a feel for the suffering that comes from leading without control. His letters to the Corinthians, especially the second, lay bare the suffering he felt in the absence of control.

And, besides other things, I am under daily pressure because of my anxiety for all the churches.

2 CORINTHIANS 11:28

The pathos of Paul's letters will hopefully comfort you. Rest assured, you are in good company. And more, we hear over and over how our suffering for Christ is a true blessing.

And not only that, but we also boast in our sufferings, knowing that suffering produces endurance, and endurance produces character, and character produces hope, and hope does not disappoint us, because God's love has been poured into our hearts through the Holy Spirit that has been given to us.

ROMANS 5:3–5

Think of your calling to spiritual adventure as a challenge to put together a puzzle from random pieces. You've been trained and conditioned to construct the puzzle in a certain way, beginning with the edge pieces first, then moving on to the pieces with the most definition, and so on. Just don't let anyone else help you because they will mess you up!

But while you are busily completing the puzzle, our Lord is also at work, putting the same pieces together in a way completely unknown to you. His way, not yours. He'll use the same pieces, but His approach will be radically different and the final picture in the puzzle will not be the one you expected.

You never really had control over the puzzle. Yes, you thought you did, and you were told that you did, because you were trained to do it the world's way. But our Lord's way is better and will lead to glory untold. You may put the puzzle together with great speed and efficiency, maybe even with some flair. But His way is the way of love and yes, suffering, both His and yours. His picture will be a picture of perfect love. Embrace His way and find your place in His puzzle picture.

The Gospel gives our suffering personal and cosmic meaning,
by connecting our pain to the pain of others and, finally,
by connecting us to the very pain of God.
RICHARD ROHR

4
THE SUN, MOON, AND STARS

Lord I regularly find myself underestimating You. Intellectually
I understand that You are greater than I can imagine. But in most of my daily
experiences I invariably shove You to the background. I guess I just haven't
learned how to live in/with You and I haven't given You center
stage in all things. Please forgive me. Amen.

I magine if you will, a cosmos with only the sun to occupy our sky. No
moon, no stars, no planets, or comets. The nighttime sky is nothing but
blackness: dark space stretching from horizon to horizon, into a seeming
eternity of emptiness.

Consider the psychological impact of never knowing what is "out
there" and of knowing only darkness and void. Expressions like "reach
for the stars" would never have existed, nor would lyrics like "when you
wish upon a star." Not to mention the all-time classic "Blue Moon." We
could go on.

He brought him outside and said, "Look toward heaven
and count the stars, if you are able to count them." Then he said to him,
"So shall your descendants be."
GENESIS 15:5

And what's more, we'd never know the size of our universe, its origins or the wonder of galaxies, pulsars, red giants, black holes, and the other amazing creations—many of which continue to baffle us. Any sense of bigness would be profoundly diminished. And humanity's desire to explore, to see what's out there would be equally stunted.

When I look at your heavens, the work of your fingers, the moon and the stars that you have established; what are human beings that you are mindful of them, mortals that you care for them?
PSALM 8:3-4

Perhaps we'd have a lesser view of even God Himself. What kind of God would plant His children alone in the darkness of space? A creator who surrounded us with an interminable sea of darkness might not be so benevolent.

But of course, the creation that surrounds us is anything but darkness. The night sky never ceases to inspire, awe and sometimes confound us. We feel an eternal calling to the heavens. It's in our DNA. We instinctively look up. Our creator designed us to look up. From antiquity, He has used the night sky to cradle our sense of adventure.

Can we believe that's why He did it? After all, we'll likely never actually reach the stars, at least not any time soon. Did He really do it all just for us? Just us on the tiny speck we know as the third planet from an ordinary sun in a run-of-the-mill galaxy?

Not knowing is part of the allure, part of our faith. Perhaps we don't need to understand, but simply take comfort in knowing a God who—for us—spun an incredible cosmos, literally speaking it into being, a creation whose abundance and beauty go beyond our comprehension. If our Creator might do something as extravagant as that, what else might He do?

*I'll tell you one thing about the universe, though. The universe is a
pretty big place. It's bigger than anything anyone has ever dreamed
of before. So if it's just us... seems like an awful waste of space.*

ELLIE ARROWAY IN CONTACT

So give thanks. Consider that patterns sown into your very existence
reflect the immensity and wonder of just what your Creator can do.

5
WEATHERING THE STORM

Lord, my emotions run up and down with how things are going.
When things are sunny, my demeanor is upbeat. But when storms
cloud the sky, anyone can tell just by looking at my face.
And amazingly, I am always surprised when the storm ends and
the sun reappears. Please forgive my lack of faith. Amen.

It doesn't take long to learn: storms will come: more like tornadoes than hurricanes, unpredictably appearing out of nowhere with little warning. Moving in an erratic path, they leave destruction in their wake: financial problems, legal issues, personnel crises, health challenges, and more.

It's a dangerous business, going out your door. You step onto the road, and if you don't keep your feet, there's no telling where you might be swept off to.

BILBO BAGGINS IN THE FELLOWSHIP OF THE RING

Where do you turn? Where is the safe harbor? Can you avoid the suffering that comes with the storm?

We know that Jesus calmed a storm on the Sea of Galilee. He can calm any storm, but we know that He doesn't calm them all. Some, like the Flood, must run their course.

Of all the biblical storm stories, perhaps Jonah's offers the best lesson. For Jonah actually *asked* to be thrown overboard into the teeth of a fierce storm. In the face of overwhelming adversity he placed himself in God's hands. And that is what we are called to do as well.

The storm stories in scripture are tempered by the promises of God, beginning with a rainbow. It's not so much that our prayers will always move Him to quiet every storm. Instead, God will help us weather them and see the good. Our Lord promises to be with us, to help us face anything as long as we look to Him.

But the Lord provided a large fish to swallow up Jonah;
and Jonah was in the belly of the fish three days and three nights.
JONAH 1:17

Jonah's prayer from the belly of the fish:

I called to the Lord out of my distress, and he answered me;
out of the belly of Sheol I cried, and you heard my voice.
You cast me into the deep, into the heart of the seas,
and the flood surrounded me;
all your waves and your billows passed over me.
Then I said, "I am driven away from your sight;
how shall I look again upon your holy temple?"
The waters closed in over me; the deep surrounded me;
weeds were wrapped around my head at the roots of the mountains.
I went down to the land whose bars closed upon me forever;
yet you brought up my life from the Pit, O Lord my God.
As my life was ebbing away, I remembered the Lord;
and my prayer came to you, into your holy temple.
Those who worship vain idols forsake their true loyalty.
But I with the voice of thanksgiving will sacrifice to you;
what I have vowed I will pay. Deliverance belongs to the Lord!

Be merciful to me, O God, be merciful to me, for in you
my soul takes refuge; in the shadow of your wings I will take refuge,
until the destroying storms pass by.
PSALM 57:1

6
THE BETTER PART

Lord, I get down on myself if I don't accomplish something every day.
When I look back over a period of weeks, months or years, I get the same
feeling: I could have done more. So I work harder (though not necessarily
more effectively). I feel like a hamster running in a wheel.
And yet, I know that You want me to spend more of myself with You.
I just don't know how to get off the wheel. Please forgive me. Amen.

T he tenth chapter of Luke tells the story of sisters Mary and Martha.
You know them well.

---

*But the Lord answered her, "Martha, Martha, you are worried and
distracted by many things; there is need of only one thing. Mary has chosen
the better part, which will not be taken away from her."*
LUKE 10:41-42

It is indisputable that Jesus affirmed Mary's as the "better part." Where
does that leave all of us Marthas, those of us who are so determined to
get things done? After all, we have an organization to build and goals to
meet. The people we serve need us to do more than just sit at the feet of
Jesus. We have work to do. And a reputation to uphold.

But note that Jesus didn't condemn Martha, nor did He tell her to stop
working. Note also that in the preceding paragraphs, we hear of the Good
Samaritan, one of Jesus' most quoted parables, describing a doer, a man
who acted when others failed to act.

... But Israel, who did strive for the righteousness that is based
on the law, did not succeed in fulfilling that law. Why not? Because they did
not strive for it on the basis of faith, but as if it were based on works.
They have stumbled over the stumbling stone, as it is written,
"See, I am laying in Zion a stone that will make people stumble, a rock that
will make them fall, and whoever believes in him will not be put to shame."
ROMANS 9:31-33

So how do we make any sense of the seeming contradictions? Do we sit at the feet of Jesus or do we serve?

Without love, deeds, even the most brilliant, count as nothing.
THÉRÈSE DE LISIEUX

The answer lies in our hearts. Was Martha serving out of love? Was she "worried and distracted" by the fear of looking like a bad hostess? Was she stumbling over the stone of achievement? Of perceived duty? Of reliance on works to gain approval from our Lord? Was she placing her work ahead of her Lord?

The story doesn't require us to choose. It does call us to serve, when we serve, out of faith in Christ and love for Him. And when we sit at the feet of Jesus, to likewise sit in faith in Him, and love for Him. He is to be first in all things. Any other motive leads us to worry and distraction.

So we will do both. We must do both. Christ will never condemn us for sitting at His feet and absorbing all we can from Him. Likewise, He will never condemn us for serving. He just wants to be the center of it. Either way, only He is "the better part."

7
YOUR WOUNDS

Lord, I don't wish to overplay this, but I get wounded on a daily
basis. Suffering seems to be part of this calling, from behind-the-back
gossip, angry confrontation to painful loneliness. Not only that, but past
wounds seem to arise, recalling memories I would prefer to forget.
I am not getting through this spiritual adventure unscathed.
Please forgive me for expecting too much. Amen.

Is it true? Are wounds an inevitable by-product of your spiritual
adventure?

*"Simon, Simon, listen! Satan has demanded to sift all of you like wheat, but
I have prayed for you that your own faith may not fail; and you, when once
you have turned back, strengthen your brothers."*

LUKE 22:31-32

Actually, your wounds may truly be the *point* of your spiritual adventure. Peter's wound, his three denials of Jesus, was a deep one. He wept
bitterly over it, and felt utterly disconnected from his Lord. But like Peter,
you may be asked, after you have "turned back," to use your wound to
"strengthen your brothers."

In Love's service, only wounded soldiers can serve.
BRENNAN MANNING

Your wounds, past and present, are sensitizers to the pain of others. Without your wounds and the scars you bear, you'd have little ability to console, empathize and help heal the wounds of others. Your wounds are your ticket into the pain of the world.

He jests at scars that never felt a wound.
ROMEO, ROMEO AND JULIET

As a Christian leader you are called to freely expose and share your wounds. They give you a unique gift: the power to be in communion with those you serve and with those who serve with you. In fact, you are powerless to lead from the (false) image that you have made it through life unscathed by suffering and defeat.

The great illusion of leadership is to think that man can be led out of the desert by someone who has never been there.
HENRI NOUWEN

The beauty of sharing your wounds is that doing so creates community. It breaks down walls of loneliness and offers hope, for you as well as for others. Hiding behind a false wall of impregnability isolates you from literally everyone, including your true self.

The paradox of Christian leadership is that the way out is the way in, that only by entering into communion with human suffering can relief be found.
HENRI NOUWEN

Your greatest model is Christ Himself: who suffered and died, and who shares His scars with all who will commune with Him.

AFTERWORD

"Your calling from God is where your gifts intersect with the world's needs."

This quote, or some variation of it, has become a mantra for many who would decline any calling that falls outside of their self-imposed comfort zone. When combined with the overwhelming nature of the world's needs, it is easy to see why so many can be found hiding behind this unscriptural expression. *"I feel the need but I am just not gifted in that. It's too much for one person. Maybe someone else will act."*

Of course, a calling that demands more than we can offer *is*, in fact, scriptural: few figures in scripture escaped the feeling that God was calling them to the impossible or the undesirable or the unknown. And of course, that's precisely what God wants. As Paul tells us repeatedly, God's callings are designed to keep us from boasting about what we've accomplished, giving the glory to him alone: it's God working in us that makes it all possible.

...For it is God who is at work in you, enabling you both to will and to work for his good pleasure.
PHILIPPIANS 2:13

And as to the overwhelming nature of the world's needs, we simply cannot allow ourselves to be intimidated to the extent that we fail to take even one small step.

...Sometimes the devil gives us great desires
so that we will avoid setting ourselves to the task at hand,
serving our Lord in possible things.
TERESA OF ÀVILA

So what does God expect of us? To rise above our limited gifts and achieve great things? To solve problems that have plagued mankind for generations?

It's really simple: He calls us to say "yes" to Him. To be willing to take the first step outside our comfort zone. Nothing more. Just engage in God's calling and let Him show you what He can do with that tiny seed that He has planted deep inside you.

Take that step. Meet our Lord in the claim that He has placed on your life from the beginning of time. When you do, I promise that you will experience Him like never before. That is my prayer for you.

NOTES ON QUOTES

An important part of my spiritual awakening was the discovery of authors who have written with special insight and depth. In a way, they have become friends and mentors to me through their words, accompanying me as I travel the pilgrim's road.

So it was natural for me to liberally quote these deep thinkers of the faith. The Roman Catholic Church calls them "doctors" of the faith, and I quite agree. Mother Teresa was not, and despite not having a significant body of published work, I turn to her words often for strength.

I have great respect for Fr. Richard Rohr, a Franciscan priest and founder of the Center for Action and Contemplation. He has written a number of books and is a widely quoted speaker. I have a special regard for his insight in the following books:

- *Everything Belongs*
- *The Naked Now*
- *Falling Upward*
- *Immortal Diamond*

Henri Nouwen was a master in getting the most out of few words. His books are deep and typically short, readable in one or two sessions. My library includes the following Nouwen books:

- *The Wounded Healer*
- *The Genesee Diary*
- *Spiritual Direction*
- *With Burning Hearts*
- *The Road to Daybreak*
- *The Way of the Heart*
- *Life of the Beloved*
- *Heart Speaks to Heart*
- *Finding My Way Home*
- *The Return of the Prodigal Son*

I have also been greatly influenced by mystics of the past. In particular, the *Cloud of Unknowing*, and the *Book of Privy Counseling*, written by an anonymous fourteenth century author and edited by William Johnston, is must reading for any seeker into contemplative thinking. This book was especially helpful to me in structuring and disciplining my writing.

Finally, the sixteenth century produced two reformers/authors whose thoughts are and will forever be relevant to our faith. Those authors, Teresa of Àvila and St. John of the Cross, have influenced the faith of millions, including mine. You can get a taste of their insights in *The Dark Night of the Soul,* by Gerald G. May.

SPIRITUAL ENTRPRENEURS IN SCRIPTURE

You may be interested to know about the spiritual entrepreneurs mentioned in this book. They come from every era of our faith history, and from varied backgrounds. While it may appear that they have very little in common, there is at least one thing that they do have in common: they were all unlikely choices for entrepreneurship.

The following are, to my mind, the most notable spiritual entrepreneurs from scripture:

Gideon: A wheat farmer, Gideon lived in a time when Israel was oppressed by the Midianites and Amalekites. Gideon was called by God to lead an army of the Israelites in battle. Once he had assembled a large army, God pruned it down to only 300. With God's help, the 300 defeated a much larger enemy force. You can read about Gideon in the book of Judges.

Esther: Esther was a young Hebrew woman held, along with her people, in an exiled captivity. Through a series of strange circumstances, she became queen of the captor nation. During a period of persecution of the captive people, she was called upon to speak out for her people and did so at great personal risk. You can read about her in the book of Esther.

David: Considered the greatest king of Israel, David did not start out as a king-to-be. He lived in obscurity as a shepherd and the youngest son of Jesse. When the prophet Samuel visited Jesse to anoint one of his sons as the future king, Jesse did not even think of David and left him in the pasture with the sheep. Despite his nondescript background David rose to become a great warrior, poet and musician. And as king he unified Judah and Israel. You can read about David in 1 Samuel, 2 Samuel, 1 Kings and 2 Kings.

New Testament Figures: The followers of Jesus came from humble backgrounds. **Andrew, Peter, James,** and **John** were fishermen. **Matthew** was a tax collector. **Mary Magdalene** was reputed to be a prostitute. Yet all of these figures, along with **Paul, Barnabas**, **Silas, Timothy,** and a few others, became first generation leaders of the church. You can read about them in the four Gospels and also in the book of Acts.

The Gospel of John closes with these words:

But there are also many other things that Jesus did;
if every one of them were written down, I suppose that the world
itself could not contain the books that would be written.

In the 21st century, the risen Christ continues to do "many other things" for each of us as we engage with Him. My prayer for you is that this book might be only the beginning as our Lord writes the story of *your* own unique spiritual adventure. When you say "yes" to His persistent whisper, you are opening yourself to a lifetime of spiritual adventures. And indeed, the world itself could not contain the books that He will write with you.

NOTES

NOTES